saving donkey

saving donkey

Peter K. High

Saving Donkey
Published by Peter K. High
New Zealand

© 2016 Peter K. High

ISBN 978-0-473-35744-3 (Softcover)
ISBN 978-0-473-35745-0 (ePUB)
ISBN 978-0-473-35746-7 (Kindle)

Editing & Production:
Andrew Killick
andrew@safelittleworld.co.nz

Cover design:
Bryan Hefer
www.bryandesign.co.nz

Professional photography:
Terry (Divot) James

Printed in New Zealand

Contents

Preface

I originally started writing this book as some sort of legacy to leave to my adorable grandchildren. I wanted to tell them about who I am, and who I was. I wanted to share with them my adventures in life, and the love I have for riding my Harley-Davidson up and down the length of our beautiful country. The project grew a bit, so here I am presenting it to a wider audience.

The book covers a lot of ground – some interesting family history, some personal stuff about the good times and the bad, plenty of motorbike riding and some discussions about life, the universe and everything. I've taken a small amount of creative licence in telling the story. Some might say I've used my imagination in creating the JC character. But I'll leave the answer to that question up to you, the reader. I can say, though, that the thoughts expressed in the conversations with him and the characteristics of the man are, I believe, true to life as I've experienced it. This minor matter of perception aside, everything else happened pretty much exactly as I've told it.

I dedicate this book, in memory of my parents, Ken and Mando (Jean) High; to my eldest son, Stephen High; to my youngest son, Tony High; to Stephen's wife (my daughter-in-law), Jennifer (Toetu) High; to my four grandchildren, Joshua High, Litara High, Samuel High and Luke High; to my great-grandson, Chase; and to all my future great-grandchildren. Also, I especially dedicate this book to my beautiful wife, Denzil Laurence, who has filled my life with happiness, encouragement and loving security – *I believe every human being should be loved unconditionally by another human being at least once in this life.*

I would also like to thank a very close family friend, Elaine Wells, for the book she wrote on my family and the research she did, which I was able to use and which inspired me to complete this book. The story of Jean and Ken will soon be published in coffee table format.

Thanks also to my good friend, Helen Medlyn (Diva), who gave the manuscript its first punctuation haircut, and to my colleague, the designer Bryan Hefer for his artistic expertise in creating the cover.

Last, but not least, thanks to my editor, Andrew Killick, who took the chapters, sentences and words, and tuned them into this fine, flowing book. His encouraging comments on my humble linguistic skills and his discipline and research, while keeping me on track to meet deadlines, have made me appreciate the talents that helped pull this book together.

My father used to enjoy writing poetry. After he died, in

amongst his belongings, I found this poem by Dorothy Nell McDonald. It's a thought I'd like to pass on to my loved ones, and you, the reader.

I do not wish you joy without sorrow,
Nor endless days without the healing dark,
Nor brilliant sun without the restful shadow,
Nor tides that never turn against your barque.

I wish you faith and strength and wisdom and love,
God's gold enough to help life's needy ones.
I wish you songs but also blessed silence
And God's sweet peace when every day is done.

I hope you enjoy this book.

Donkey

Chapter 1

You can't fast-track experiential maturity, you can
only acquire it by living the years.

Summer was upon us, along with the holidays. A joyous time of year for some, a lonely time of year for some. I decided that, seeing the sun was out, I would hop on the Harley and cruise somewhere for a coffee.

I found myself in Orewa, on the Hibiscus Coast, north of New Zealand's largest city, Auckland, and pulled up onto the footpath, parking the bike outside a café. The beach looked inviting and just a hint of a summer breeze on the water gave the effect of several million diamonds glistening in the sun.

I must admit, I love riding a Harley; I love the sound and the image and everything about it. I've ridden many bikes in my time, but the Harley is more than a bike – it's a machine you bond with. It's a heavy beast, at around 340 kg, but, having a low centre of gravity, it's an easy bike to ride. There is one difficult thing I find about riding a Harley though – it's trying to resist looking at myself in shop windows as I ride by.

I took off my helmet and went into the café to order my coffee – a takeaway latte, single shot, with cinnamon on top. At that stage, I had only been drinking coffee for six months, which was unusual for a 60-year-old; even now, I only like coffee in a paper takeaway cup with a plastic lid. So, by then, a single shot latte was some pretty big progress from a fluffy.

Life is treating me well today, I thought. History had proven that these moments don't always last and, because of that, it was good to get a win with life and feel this way every now and then.

I sat there in the sun and reflected back on my life. I considered how fortunate I had been to have a great upbringing with loving, caring parents – a stark contrast to the lives of a lot of young people today.

My mother was Greek. Beginning life in Egypt, and brought up in Cairo by her Greek parents, she met my father during World War II when he was a dispatch rider in the New Zealand Army (motorbikes were in my blood).

Adamandia Segredos, known for much of her life as 'Jean', was born on the 3rd of July, 1926, in Mansoura, the third largest city in Egypt. One day, at the local skating rink in Cairo, she met a young New Zealander called Ken High. He asked her name and, because she had been told by her family not to talk to soldiers (and because Adamandia was hard to pronounce), she said, 'Jean.' She claimed this was the only fib she ever told my father.

To her family, she was affectionately known as 'Mando'.

Her parents, Petros and Christina Segredos, came from the little Greek island of Sikinos. Mando was the youngest of three children, with her sister, Anna (Nini), being fourteen years her senior, and Nicholas, her brother, being twelve years older.

Mando was just sixteen when she and Ken were married. Two years into their marriage, Mando developed chronic glaucoma. During the war, the British Army drew away the entire supply of general anaesthetic from Cairo's local hospitals; so the many operations which Mando had to endure on her eyes were conducted without a general anaesthetic. This proved too much for her to endure and, in the following years, she gave up on treatment and eventually became totally blind.

In 1944, Ken was seconded to work in administration at Headquarters, 2nd New Zealand Expeditionary Force, in London, and so the family moved to Britain. Not long after, a daughter, Dorothy, was born to Mando and Ken, but she was tragically killed when a plane crashed into the building next door to the family home.

On the 1st of February, 1946, the family left London's Tilbury Docks aboard the hospital ship *Maunganui*, bound for New Zealand, via the Suez Canal. They docked at Port Said and, there to greet them, just as they had arranged, were Mando's mother and father, her sister, Nini, her brother-in-law, Joseph (with their baby daughter, Lucy), Mando's brother, Nicholas, and his wife, who was also called Mando.

For the few hours that the ship was in port, the family dined out at a hotel together. The occasion was both happy and sad. Happy, because they were all together; sad, because they had no idea when they might see each other again. It was an emotional farewell. Mando's father, Petros, was crying as they said their goodbyes. He loved his youngest daughter dearly, but he knew in his heart that her place was with her husband – even if that place was on the other side of the world. Her father's parting words to her were, 'I will never see you again.' Mando said to him, 'Don't be silly, of course you will see me again'; but he never did. The last vision my mother had of her father was of him running up the wharf beside the ship, waving and crying.

Mando and Ken settled in Dunedin, in the South Island of New Zealand; their first home was in the transit camp at Tomahawk Beach, south of the city. It was there they met their lifelong friends, the Maxwells. From the camp, they moved to 60 Mayfield Avenue in Wakari, and that is where I was born. Nine years after me, Paul was born.

Moving from Dunedin many years later, Ken and Jean (as Mando was known in New Zealand) took early retirement in Motueka. They stayed there for twenty years, until Ken developed Parkinson's and I moved them to Auckland so that they would be closer to me. Jean had established a connection with Dunedin and New Zealand culture. Even when living in Auckland, her loyalty always remained with Otago Rugby, and her walking frame created much amusement, sporting its Otago Highlanders flag on one side and All Blacks flag on the other.

My mother, though small in stature, had a blusterous personality. Because she was blind, she had to learn English by ear, phonetically. This created constant amusement for us, because she was forever butchering the English language as she struggled to get her points of view (of which she had many) across.

Some of her favourite inadvertent linguistic errors included: 'Oh, you have a dirty concert,' when she meant, 'Oh, you have a guilty conscience.' Reflecting on her marriage, she would say, 'Oh, Ken and I were very happy, but we had our upside-downs' (ups and downs). A real brain-teaser for us was when she said, 'Pristikis don't care.' We later found out it was, 'Cheats never prosper.' A popular stand-in for being 'two-faced' was, 'You're just second-hand faces.' Another mis-saying was 'kick a bucket' (kicked the bucket).

On one occasion, a neighbour asked my mother what team I was playing at rugby that week. My mother couldn't remember the name and finally said, 'You know. Two bones and a dead head.' The team was The Pirates, who displayed the skull and crossbones on their shirts. Then there was the woman my mother knew who had just married a younger man – my mother describing him as the woman's 'dolly man' (toy boy).

When the yachtsman Russell Coutts defected from the Team New Zealand America's Cup sailing crew, my mother called him a 'Judith' (Judas). 'Stacey' was a name she couldn't say, so after various attempts at referring to league great, Stacey Jones, as 'Chesty', she finally settled for 'Jonesy'. The All Black legend, Tana Umaga, also proved too much of a mouthful and was often referred to as 'Tara Moana'.

One day, my mother fell and broke some bones in her

foot and, for a while, was confined to a wheelchair in a local hospital. I would visit her and often she sat in the lounge with other older folk. The wheelchairs were parked in a semicircle like wagons around a campfire. The other patients were in various states of mental ability and were mostly content to just sit and stare and say nothing. My blind mother said to me, 'Pete, is there anyone else here?'

'Yes,' I said, 'the lounge is full.'

'What's wrong with them?' she responded. 'Why don't they say something? Are they waiting with the fairies?' (Away with the fairies.)

In her latter years, my mother was unfortunately confined to a rest home. I used to visit and spend time with her, working from her room on my laptop. One day, I arrived at the rest home and they had an entertainer there with his guitar, singing all the old favourites. I could hear my mother's loud, out-of-tune voice drowning out even the entertainer as she sang along, because – being blind – she had no idea who else was in the room. I must admit, I was guilty of hiding outside the door on the odd occasion until they had finished a song, before I stepped in and whisked her away.

Even in her prime, my mother only stood approximately 138 cm tall. In fact, she was – as I used to tease her – '138 cm round'. I swear she would almost rock herself back to sleep just trying to sit up in the morning.

From a very early age, my mother instilled great positive affirmation in me.

She would constantly pinch my cheek and say, 'Petros,

my big handsome boy, you are so clever.' I grew up believing this, and I felt I was better and smarter than my peers.

I was always a little guy, but I didn't realise I was small and, although I didn't excel, I punched well above my weight in sport and life. It wasn't until I got to the doubting teens that I began to question myself. At school, I began to develop excuses to cover for being a lazy learner with a short attention span.

There was a growing awareness in society about how conditions at home could affect a child's performance at school, and some of us were smart enough to make use of that trend. I noticed that some kids would talk about how their father was mean to them, or he was a drunk, or their mother had left them, and the system always allowed these kids more leeway. I had a perfect excuse of my own to call on as justification for not doing well at school – my mother was blind, and this, supposedly, put a lot of pressure on me. I endeavoured to milk that angle for all it was worth.

Fortunately, however, my excuses and 'pity-parties', along with the negative behavioural trend I was trying to develop, couldn't compete with the positive affirmation that my mother had instilled in me from an early age, and I succeeded in life – in spite of myself.

As in everyone's life, I was thrown the odd curve ball. Paul, my younger brother, was killed on his motorcycle at the age of fifteen, and my mother never got over it. There was something in her Greek upbringing and culture that meant she never *wanted* to get over it. This was the only time my mother ever let me down.

Mando had the not-so-good habit of rating friends and family, and had to have favourites. My brother had become her favourite, and I was fine with that because I was married by this time with two sons – one of whom she had made another of her favourites.

When my brother died, my mother was, to put it mildly, 'hysterically absorbed in grief' – and I'm talking uncontrollable sorrow. She turned on me one day with the typical Greek open-hand gesture and screamed, 'Why? Why?' I told her that I didn't know. Then, with equal passion she looked at me again and said, 'Why was it him? Why wasn't it you?'

Initially stunned, I quickly dismissed the encounter as the ravings of an overwrought and terribly upset woman. I admit, though, later in life, during a period of self-pity, I tried to milk my mother's words as an excuse for non-performance in life. But, once again, the positive affirmation from my mother in my *early* life triumphed, and I quickly got over it.

That disturbing interaction with my mother, and my brother's death, made me realise how fragile relationships are. These things made me question who we can really trust with our deepest, most sensitive emotions. People, unfortunately, will let us down. They don't always do it intentionally, but they're not always there when we need them most. That sense of loss is keen when people close to us die; they're suddenly not there when we need them – not, of course, through any fault of their own or of ours (we would hope not anyway).

Despite playing favourites, my mother loved me like

mothers do, but she was human as well, with all the confused frailties of a distressed person.

As I sat in that Orewa café, deep in contemplation, I realised that my life had been a series of peaks and valleys and twists and turns. I guess it's this type of emotional terrain that shapes our characters one way or the other, for good or for bad. I always referred to this as 'experiential maturity' and attributed any success I attained to getting older and wiser. Now, as I approached the age of sixty-one, I knew that this understanding was only partly true. I knew you couldn't fast-track experiential maturity, you could only acquire it by living the years.

Chapter 2

Under my T-shirt sleeve is a tattoo of my past lives. It is a heart with five names in it, all crossed out, one after the other. It not only reveals my past lives but, more specifically, it lists the names of my past wives. It's a great talking point, and I always dismiss it by saying, 'It's only because my first five wives didn't like me. It was nothing to do with me.' (Said tongue in cheek, of course.) I had reached a certain point in life where I had decided that, the next time I found a woman who didn't like me, I should just go ahead and give her a house – up front – to save myself all the other pain, sadness and financial hardship. I used to think marriage was like an alarm clock – you got a ring, then you woke up!

My wives were – and remain – very nice ladies. There's only one I still don't particularly like as a person. She was, in my opinion, rather ruthless – a bit like Colonel Gaddafi with highlights – but that was a long time ago. (Now, that's got the other four guessing!)

I have come to understand some general points of wisdom through my experience.

1. The first marriage is usually the easiest to work at and protect.
2. The two biggest causes of marriage break-up are sex and money – usually a lack of one or both.
3. Insecurity, for a woman, is usually a greater 'sin' than infidelity. My understanding is that if a guy has an affair and his wife finds out, she will make his life hell but, more often than not, she won't leave. I think sometimes she will hang on in there so she can continue to punish him. However, should a man threaten the family finances, he's toast!

Obviously, security wasn't my strong point. I was a loyal husband, but I was a risk-taker and gambled on projects, often hiding them from my spouse. One of my wives, who was a lovely person, struggled with the insecurity of the financial peaks and valleys I created. Her main fault was having superior wisdom in hindsight. She could always predict the future… all twenty-seven different possible outcomes… *after* the event. Of course, with those odds, one was *sure* to be right! Inevitably!

I knew that, when a big risk paid off, it would normally reap a big reward; but if it failed, then failure would be failure. If I wasn't able to hide a big risk from my wife, then I would only be permitted – at best – to take half a risk. To my mind, this would only reap me half a reward. The problem was, my life was a journey through the law of averages – I needed those big rewards to get me through the times of failure.

I completely understood her reasons for leaving. As we all know, when a spouse leaves, all assets are divided – halved – so that added to my money struggles. Meanwhile, I noticed that when finances were good – which was more often than not – my wives were happy to stay and enjoy the good times that the money provided.

I am by no means a wealthy man (well, not these days anyway), but in the outcomes of divorce settlements, I decided to simply 'gift' the money, without seriously contesting anything, and move on. It's only money and, quite frankly, I believe most of us never feel really wealthy anyway – we're always just going through different levels of being broke!

This leads me back to the question I raised in the previous chapter – who can we truly trust with our emotions?

Our kids? Up until they're teenagers, they need to trust us with their emotions – but we sure can't trust them. When they've grown, they have their own families and – understandably – their priorities change. And, anyway, young people are tricky. They say that they're leaving home, but they come back! More often than not, with a little dog. Then, they leave again and leave the dog behind. I had a friend who brought a friend home, then left – leaving his friend behind. His friend lived with my friend's parents for over a decade, and even started calling them Mum and Dad!

As I sat in Orewa, I started to think about when I was a solo dad, at the age of 28, with my two sons Stephen (7) and Tony (5). It was the late 1970s and there weren't many solo dads in those days. It wasn't long after we had moved to the Wellington area that my first wife left the marriage. She and I had married young, and she fell in love with her boss. They are still married to this day. Almost from the day she left, and through the ensuing years, the boys, unfortunately, didn't maintain good contact with their mother – even though they would have liked to have kept in touch. Being kids, they didn't make a great effort, and so it was easy for their mother to see herself as the neglected victim. But she could have tried a lot harder. It was all a bit messy really, and everything could have been handled better by everyone – me included.

I remember when she told us she was going. The boys were so upset, they cried their little hearts out. I thought they would never stop. But I began to notice how well kids adapt. When they got hungry, they stopped crying to eat. After food, they would cry their little hearts out again. Then their favourite TV show would come on, and they would stop crying to watch that. I, on the other hand, would be too upset to eat and certainly didn't feel like watching TV. I think adults can learn a lot from our kids about coping.

I found, as a young disorganised person, that I had to get organised. Everything had to be done – we had no microwave or dryer – just an old ringer washing machine and a normal stove. I ended up with maybe twenty chores to do a day – and I got them done. I learnt to work smart. I soon realised you cannot do the breakfast dishes the night before to save time in the morning!

This solo parent responsibility enabled me to appreciate housework. I realised that, in most cases, it didn't matter how these chores were divided between a couple, the responsibility for ensuring they were done to a high standard still fell, somewhat unfairly, upon the female. Because of this, I was looked on as a poor guy struggling to cope on his own, bringing up two young boys; so the quality of my housework wasn't expected to be as high as that of a woman in similar circumstances. It was easier in those days for a guy to go out on his own, because people afforded me allowances which solo mums – through no fault of their own – didn't receive. I still appreciate that being a working mum is a major task.

Meanwhile, the company that I was working for was worried about my ability to look after my kids and the business. For them, reaching my sales budgets took priority. My boss actually gave me an ultimatum – my kids or my job. I chose both and performed well, breaking sales records and stabilising a territory that had previously turned over ten sales reps in two years.

As time moved on, the kids got older and were able to assist me with minor chores around the house. I bought an automatic washing machine when they came out, and a dryer and microwave. My chores reduced from twenty a day to five a day – but I still didn't seem to have any spare time. Somehow, I just seemed to drag those five chores out over the same period of time that it took me to complete the twenty. Funny that.

I have always made light of my past. Let's face it – very

few people have the crossed-out names of the five loves of their lives tattooed, one after the other, inside a heart on their arm. I should have mentioned earlier that, under the crossed-out names, the tattoo reads, 'Harley-Davidson Forever'. I usually qualify this statement by saying, 'I found the Harley quieter.' Depending on the company, I sometimes add, 'and it doesn't weigh as much.' This happy-go-lucky attitude of mine helped get me through the heartache we all experience when love ends, whether we be the leaver or the 'leavee'.

Recently, I had a rotator cuff operation and, as I was coming out of the anaesthetic, I could hear the nurses discussing my tattoo. I was just regaining consciousness, and it sounded as if they were speaking into a 200-litre metal drum, the sound of their voices swirling around my head at various pitches.

I could hear one saying, 'This guy has his five ex-wives tattooed on his arm.'

Another said, 'Truly?'

'Yeah, look.'

'Huh, he has too.'

Then one said, 'What's so special about him that he's had all these women marrying him?'

Although I was still too sedated to speak, I do remember feeling a little concerned that they may have been peeking under the sheets!

I invariably use humour in testing situations as an opportunity to create a stalling effect, giving me time to get my head around what is happening and to plan my next move. My unexpected jocularity will often throw the other party, and encourage them to react. In this way, I am able to assess their stance and/or thoughts, and so determine what I will do next. Right or wrong, it's a technique I developed over the years.

Another strategy I developed in debates and argumentative situations, is the theory that if my opponent had instigated the disagreement, they would – more often than not – project their strongest argument up front. Normally, this would be their best shot – so I established a set of generic answers, which they wouldn't expect, to counter. Just like in an old western, I would count on them only having one bullet in the chamber. Once fired, their six-gun would be empty. Then, to the imaginary soundtrack of 'click, click' from their now useless weapon, I would prepare to fire my next round.

Another old western strategy I cultivated was, instead of engaging my opponents, I would sometimes imagine turning my horse around and riding away as fast as I could, while firing the odd shot over my shoulder – just enough to keep them at bay. It was a technique that required confidence – well, *perceived* confidence at least.

Once again, I can't help thinking about how that self-confidence of mine, having been implanted in me as a child by my mother, reinforces the importance of positive affirmation by parents to their offspring. My blind mother only saw me – in her words – as a 'furry blob'. She meant to say 'fuzzy blur'. Some people used to say that 'furry blob' was actually a pretty accurate description and that I hadn't changed much! But my mother always meant it affectionately. Being Greek, I am very hairy. One wife claimed she awoke in the morning nearly choking on hair balls. She was always threatening to vacuum the bed…

In contrast to my mother seeing only the best in me, my father felt he had the responsibility of keeping my feet firmly on the ground and would often highlight my faults. He was, however, very supportive in one area of my life – my sport – and his encouragement continued into the next generation. My mother and father and I used to go to watch my youngest son, Tony, play schoolboy rugby. My father would lead my mother up and down the sideline, following the game. This way, when Tony was running with the ball, she could hear the other spectators yelling, 'Go Tony, go Tony!' and she would join in. When she heard the spectators roar and clap, she would do the same, realising her youngest grandson had scored a try (which he would often do). Those are the kind of memories you treasure most when you look back at life.

Chapter 3

Good God, you ride a Harley

Back to the café.

I sat outside in the sun and enjoyed my coffee. There were a few bikes riding by, which I acknowledged as they cruised past. Then I heard the sweet sound of another Harley-Davidson as it approached. The rider pulled in, with deliberate purpose, right beside my bike, as if he knew I was there and that we had a pre-planned meeting.

The Harley was a Springer, immaculate in every detail; the rider and bike looked well-suited. It was hard to pick the man's age, but he cut a very striking figure as he alighted and took off his helmet. He gave his medium-length hair a little flick, and it seemed to respond and settle where it was meant to. I thought, 'I wish I could do that.' My thick, black, Greek hair had thinned considerably over the years and was now very thin and grey.

He wandered over to me, held out his hand and said, 'Hiya, Donkey, they call me JC.'

I said, 'Hi, JC,' and thought, *This is embarrassing, I don't recall meeting this guy before.* Although, his warm smile and friendly demeanour put me well at ease.

Having ridden a Harley for a number of years, and having been involved with the Auckland HOG Chapter during that time, it wasn't unusual for people to remember me – my nickname of 'Donkey' is pretty memorable. Mind you, the stranger might just have read it off my bike – it was written on my windscreen!

I had earned my nickname because I always carried other people's gear in my saddlebags. Riders and/or their pillion passengers – whether they be wives, girlfriends, daughters, aunties or mothers – were always grateful when I could take their excess baggage. This, coupled with a supposed similarity to the wise-cracking Donkey from the film *Shrek*, caused the name to stick. Many people imagined I was called Donkey for other reasons, but that assumption usually ended in disappointment – as my five ex-wives might testify!

JC ordered his coffee and sat with me. I asked him where he was from and he smiled and said, 'Everywhere and here and there.' We talked about our bikes, and he seemed to know as much about my 2009 Softail Heritage Classic as I did, plus more. The conversation was like no other. I found myself asking all the questions and felt a strong prompt from him to keep asking.

'So…' I said, 'what does JC stand for?'

Without a flinch, he replied, 'Whatever you want it to stand for. John Clough will do.'

I have a good friend by that name and it wasn't him. Normally at this stage I would have thought, *Whoa, here's a nutter*; I would have gradually closed our conversation and ridden off. But, there was a certain genuine, open honesty in his response, and he portrayed a kind of uniqueness, which was intriguing. Anyway, he didn't look like your usual nutcase. Not only did he cut a fine figure to the point of being daunting, but he commanded respect through his presence. I felt both comfortable and curious.

'So…' I said again, 'I thought you were going to say Jesus Christ.'

He laughed with a big mischievous grin, 'Could be,' and went on to say that he knew a lot about Jesus Christ, adding that Jesus could well be in this world.

'What about other worlds?' I said, trying to give the impression I was okay with the topic of conversation, although I was conscious that other people might be listening in, and I felt a little uneasy.

'Well,' he said, 'there are no other worlds as you know them, but in the flesh I am who I said I am.'

It was all very mysterious but I seemed to grasp what he was getting at. 'So… you could be God in the flesh?'

'Could be,' he said again, laughing away.

'Then,' I said, 'why didn't you just appear as God?'

He explained that maybe if he appeared as God, then all that is around would no longer exist, because God doesn't tolerate sin and this world is full of sin. 'And, if I came as the Holy Spirit, well, that would have just freaked you and everyone else out,' he said laughingly. I wasn't sure if he was joking or not, as he didn't give any indication either way.

I was amazed where this conversation was heading.

Within minutes of meeting this guy we were discussing things that are usually considered a no-go zone between strangers; but I thought, *What the heck.* I looked at him with a grin and asked him to tell me more about Jesus Christ.

Still smiling broadly and with enthusiastic excitement, he explained that when you commit your life to Jesus you are saved from eternal death. I was still uncomfortable every time he mentioned Jesus and looked around to see if anyone had overheard him. He went on to say that when Jesus died that day over two thousand years ago, He died taking on all your sins – past, present and future. The future sins that have been forgotten are what are important, because – as God observes this world now – He doesn't see your sin, He sees the face of His Son, which is sinless. When you are a Christian, the Son purifies your existence because you believe in Him. So, in God's eyes, you are sinless, and you and the Son deal with the process of your actual purification. Then he laughed again and took a sip of his coffee.

I thought through his words. I had always considered myself a Christian – albeit not a very good one. I had committed my life to Jesus Christ while watching a Billy Graham Crusade on my parents' old Philips TV set many years ago. My memory distracted me as I recalled those old television sets – they always seemed to require a good whack on the side with an open hand to get sharper reception; and when you turned them off, they would go 'poof' and the picture would disappear into a single little light in the middle of the screen that would linger for a few seconds before disappearing completely.

I shook myself out of my daydream and made the conscious decision to focus on not wasting the opportunity of talking with this interesting fellow biker. Then I realised that if he was who he said he might be – Jesus Christ – then perhaps in some mystical way time shouldn't be an issue.

To me, a Christian is someone with all the failings common to this world, but who believes in Jesus Christ and believes that Jesus died to save us from our sins. I compare my belief about being a Christian to being a builder who builds houses, some of which may leak a bit or need some extra work. He's still a builder, just not always a very good one. To be a good person and walk what we consider a 'Christian walk', doing all the right things, is just that – a Christian *walk* and nothing more. That's fine, but you have to believe in Jesus Christ to be an actual Christian.

JC then got up and said, 'Let's ride a while. Matakana for another coffee was your next step right?'

I must have mentioned that in conversation, I thought, as the *Twilight Zone* TV theme echoed around in my head.

We put on our helmets and jackets and headed north. I was leading and felt quite nervous. I remember thinking, *If he is the Son of God, should I open the Harley up like I would normally do? This is worse than having a cop tailing you!*

The traffic was heavy as holidaymakers flocked to the beaches. I managed to cut through the traffic, jinking in and out and lane splitting, eliminating the queue of stationary vehicles that had formed a kilometre out of Matakana.

I parked up, and JC pulled in beside me. We ordered our new round of coffee and sat at a table in the courtyard.

Trying to grasp an angle on this guy who called himself JC, I mentioned that I had pushed 130/140 kph as I was passing cars on the open road, and I asked him how he viewed this law-breaking. He said that I was free to do what I wanted, but to remember that what I want and do, when it is based on my own desires, isn't always good for me. I asked him how God viewed my flouting of the road rules, and JC reminded me that God doesn't see my indiscretions because, being a born-again Christian, my future sins have already been forgiven and forgotten – God only sees the sinless face of His Son.

I casually pointed out that he must have been speeding to keep up with me.

'Was I? It's true that I arrived at the same time as you.'

Okay, I thought, *I'm not even going to try to catch the supposed Son of God speeding.*

He told me that when I flout human laws, then I'm subject to human retribution and punishment. When you flout God's laws, then you are subject to Jesus' grace of total forgiveness. But, in saying that, there can still be consequences. Total forgiveness and the consequences of your actions are two different things. That statement worried me a bit.

I had struggled over the years with mounting indiscretions and how to make amends. He said that if I wronged someone, then I can attempt to put it right to the best of my abilities. If you wrong God, then Jesus' instant and future forgiveness allows you to move on and He doesn't keep records.

He went on to say that when Jesus was crucified on the Cross, He had two thieves, one on either side of Him, who both cursed and rebuked Him for no reason other than the fact that they were afraid and angry. One later came to his senses and asked for forgiveness, asking if he could be remembered when Jesus was with the Father. He was forgiven instantly.

'What could he have done if Jesus had insisted he make amends first?' I asked. With a hint of a wry smile, JC said, 'The thief could have made all kinds of promises and had the best intentions about making amends – but he was kind of stuck in that moment. How could he have made amends if he couldn't get down from the cross? The amazing thing is, he was forgiven despite this because the grace of Jesus doesn't require retribution for sins.

'Anyway, it's such a great day, let's continue riding,' JC said. 'Plus, it will give you a chance to digest what we've talked about. Next stop, Mangawhai, and take the Wayby Valley turnoff before Wellsford as the traffic will be light and you won't have to take any more unnecessary risks dodging cars.'

I turned my back and jovially rolled my eyes at the thought of the Son of God predicting traffic congestion.

We geared up and cruised over the undulating hills towards the little, but popular, seaside town of Mangawhai Beach. I was 'coffeed out' by this stage, so we parked down by the beach and sat under a tree in the cool of the shade.

I told JC that he was surprisingly youthful-looking for a very old God. He smiled and said. 'Could be, but ageing is directly related to sin, as man and woman were designed to live forever.' He explained that God gave Adam a choice and said Adam could eat of any tree in the garden, except from the tree of the knowledge of good and evil. If he ate from this, he would surely die. Adam was tempted and eventually died. God cannot lie. He lives under His own natural law for our benefit, so Adam – who was designed to live forever – ultimately expired. From that moment, the ageing process took effect and the human lifespan decreased.

JC continued, 'However, Adam and Eve and mankind dying wasn't a punishment for this original sin. It was the consequence of Adam and Eve's actions. You see, that tree was the tree of the knowledge of good and evil, and this knowledge proved to be too much for mankind. Look at the collapse of the world's standards and morals. If life on this earth didn't end with each generation, the deterioration of future generations would continue on top of the corruption of past generations. Each generation would have its own 'Groundhog Day', happening simultaneously with every *other* generation, past, present and future.

'Remember the Cold War that was instigated during your parents' generation? On one hand, you had the Soviet Union with enough nuclear bombs to blow the world up twenty times over and, on the other hand, you had the United States of America with enough bombs to blow the world up thirty times. How ridiculous, when once would have been enough. Now, if that generation had continued to live on and not die, the nuclear war would no doubt have occurred, and people would have had to live through maiming, pain, starvation and suffering with no relief in sight. Imagine being so thirsty, yet not having anything to drink, day in, day out. Then, imagine if your generation came along to live alongside that existing generation, slapping its own screw-ups on the world. And, let's not forget that this would all happen on top of past generations' catastrophes from the beginning of time. Dying is for man's benefit, not God's. If you didn't have the deaths of past generations, you would be in a terrible state. *Dying is God's reset button for mankind...'*

JC then went on to tell me about Abraham, for he, like other biblical characters, was an interesting fellow, who had great faith and great doubts.

Abraham was born under the name Abram, in the city of Ur in Babylonia. According to Jewish tradition, he was the son of Terah, an idol merchant but, from his early childhood, he questioned the faith of his father. He came to believe that the entire universe was the work of a single Creator, and he began to teach this belief to others. (Source: Judaism 101, www.jewfaq.org)

God promised that Abraham would become the father of a nation. Abraham believed God, but he and his wife Sarah were unable to have children. The years passed.

When Sarah's faith in God's promise began to wane and she felt, at 90, that she was past child-bearing age, she suggested that her husband should sleep with their Egyptian servant Hagar, so that Abraham could have descendants. Although this led to the birth of Ishmael, it had not been God's best plan for Abraham and Sarah. Ishmael's descendants today are the people of Islam.

After JC had finished, his earlier words came back to me – that I am free to do what I want, but what I want isn't always good for me. I guess this was very applicable to Abraham. But God was good to Abraham. He and Sarah miraculously had a child of their own, and Isaac became the father of the nation of Israel.

I asked JC how important and relevant the Old Testament is in this day and age. He said that it is very pertinent and that, even though the Law of Moses no longer applies in the same context as it did in the Old Testament, it is still the benchmark – the standard – of right and wrong. 'Take Ecclesiastes, for example,' he said, 'there wouldn't be a person on this earth who wouldn't be able to relate to Solomon's battle with himself.' I recalled how, in Ecclesiastes, Solomon called his frustration 'a chasing after the wind'. I can always relate to that. The sun comes up in the morning, just to go down again at night; the rain falls into the rivers and the rivers flow into the sea, yet the sea is never full, for the process starts all over again (a chasing after the wind).

JC said that the Old Testament is a very accurate account of the people of Israel, and he said that God had designed it that way. The Jewish people kept this detailed diary of their history, warts and all, not sanitising it. They recorded their mistakes and failures – which were many – along with their successes; this gives the book credibility with scholars and non-academics alike. If the book was fictional, then it would have been censored, with only the successes being recorded; but many embarrassing and tragic stories, and numerous mistakes in the people's history, have been preserved within it. They stand as great lessons to be learned for future generations.

'Okay,' said JC, 'time to call it a day. I'm heading north, you're heading south.'

I gave him a friendly pat on the shoulder and said, 'Do we catch up again while I'm alive?' I grinned.

He said that if I was keen, we could ride some of the country together and that he would be at BP Connect Service Centre, Drury, at 9 a.m., Monday week. With that he rode off.

Riding home, the sceptic in me was strong, querying who this 'JC' really was. Although, that didn't bother me as much as the state of my mind, which was racing almost to the point of hyperventilation.

I was trying to recollect everything that had happened and was amazed how calm I had been as I had spoken with this stranger; how naturally the atmosphere between us had developed, and how the flow of conversation had been so informative and relaxing. I was astonished that I had bought into the possibility of JC being the Son of God – which, I realised, he had never confirmed nor denied.

As the week moved on, doubts filled my mind about whether the exchange had actually happened. I questioned the feeling of total absorption in our conversation, and my thoughts from the time I had been with JC began to wane.

Chapter 4

Maybe I have come to help you from the inside,
to help you help yourself – that's the way it works.

onday week came around quite quickly, and I headed south to the BP Connect Service Centre at Drury.

JC's bike was already there when I pulled in. I walked through the self-opening doors and spotted him immediately, sitting in a relaxed way – like he had all the time in the world – at one of the café tables. I waved to him and he smiled back. After ordering my single shot latte in a takeaway cup, I sat down beside him. I must admit, I was still not a 100 percent sure about whether he was some sort of divine figure – or in fact whether he even claimed to be. Everything had been pretty mysterious so far. But I liked him and wanted to trust him. I had a feeling that he was in my life for a purpose, and his answers to my questions resonated well in me.

We greeted one another. Looking out at my bike, he said, 'Glad to see you've got a full tank of gas.' I wondered how he could tell from this far away, but there was another thought in the front of my mind. Without any small talk, I asked him if he was here to help me sort my life out.

'Donks,' he said, 'your life is sorted, you just don't know it yet. Also, maybe I haven't come to help you from the outside, maybe I have come to help you from the inside, to help you help yourself – maybe that's the way it works. There was an emphasis on the 'I', which indicated to me that he was still speaking as if he was Jesus.

He went on. 'You are free to make your own choices in life, and to work towards not repeating the same mistakes. Often it's not so important what happens *to* you, but what happens *in* you. The wide path, which so many take, is cruisy in contrast to the narrow path, which can be more difficult. However, the latter has greater reward.'

I said that I understood that, but asked why it was true. He sat back in his chair, obviously preparing for an in-depth explanation.

'As much as humans often claim to like the easy way, they actually don't place much value on "easy" – they think things need to be hard to have any value. They think that if goals were easy to attain, then people would never learn the value of reaching those milestones. People use examples such as, "You wouldn't want to play in a rugby team that had no opposition would you? And you certainly wouldn't want to be a spectator. It would be like watching the All Blacks and them being the only side on the field."' He said this with a grin. He knew I could think of a few All Blacks games I'd watched where it was almost as if there hadn't been any opposition!

'Let's test this idea out,' he said. 'How hard is it to become a Christian?'

'I guess, for some, it's difficult because they have a history of being set in their old sinful ways,' I said.

'I didn't say a *good* Christian, I just said a Christian,' he replied. 'You know this answer, as it has been your principle.'

'You're right,' I said. 'My understanding is that to be a Christian you just have to believe in Jesus Christ and believe that He died to take away our sins, past, present and future.'

'Correct, but most feel they need to get their lives in order before making that commitment. However, in reality, Jesus just wants them the way they are and He will work on the rest. So… how hard is that?'

'Not hard at all,' I replied, but I knew, surprisingly, that a lot of people hadn't taken up this offer.

I thought about this from a practical point of view and saw that there was no downside. If you believe in Jesus and it's not true, then it doesn't matter. If you *don't* believe in Him and it's not true, again it doesn't matter. However, if you believe in Jesus and it's true, then you win big time. But, more importantly, if you *don't* believe and it's true, you lose big time. So, from a material, pragmatic point of view, you may as well believe. There is no 'downside'.

JC went on to say that religion had been a stumbling-block for many. God brought in laws to help humankind and, originally, people recorded them and celebrated them in appreciation of God's help and wisdom. But – over the years – a lot of these laws had become religious rituals, which had no association with the original event and detracted from the intention of the original law.

'Take circumcision, for example, which God had introduced for comfort and hygiene in the desert. (Initially, when the world was perfect, there had been no deserts. Then, during the Great Flood of Noah's time, the areas that became deserts were inundated by salt water – part of a vast ocean bottom – which then dried out as the waters receded.) These days, many of God's laws, such as circumcision, have become religious rituals that have little to do with God's original intent. These man-made rituals prevent many people from seeing God as He truly is. So – because these rites remain in, and dominate, many religions – people struggle to find God, and they give up.'

JC continued, 'Religion is man's way of trying to make things right with God through man's own efforts. Sadly, you can end up being disappointed or hating yourself, as you will fail to feel good enough to meet God's approval. The truth is, no matter what you do, you will not feel good enough. But God does not award favour on the merits of your religious deeds. That's not how He operates.

'God's law is important, but the religious side of the law should now be treated like a line drawn in the sand. Beyond it lies a memorial to a past age of how to measure right and wrong. But now Jesus' grace and forgiveness is sufficient.'

I interrupted and said, 'You mentioned that deserts were old ocean bottoms – what exactly happened there?'

'It's time to hit the road I reckon,' he said. 'Let's ride to Taupo and then talk some more there.'

My scepticism about JC was still hovering in my head, but, again, his words made sense and I found our conversations genuinely interesting.

We rode SH1 past the Rangiriri turn off, to the Tahuna Road exit. The road through to Tahuna is a great ride with little traffic. We eventually joined SH27 at the Paeroa-Tahuna Road roundabout, and continued on through to Matamata. The road was quiet with little traffic and the warm air on my face had a soothing, massage-like effect on my whole head. Dry roads and sweeping bends. This is great Harley country.

As I was riding, I was thinking about my love affair with motorbikes. My good friends, Graham and Karren, are Harley people and have a Softail Night Train. Once a year, Graham would accompany Karren to her company's Christmas function in Auckland, and he and I would catch up on the Friday and always end up at the Auckland Harley-Davidson dealership. Graham would look at the new models and I would kick some tyres.

The week after one such excursion, I was having lunch with another mate, and across the road from the restaurant was a scooter shop. We wandered over and, to cut a short story even shorter, he and I ended up buying two 50 cc scooters. We putted around Auckland for the rest of the afternoon, then had to figure out how to get our cars home. We hadn't thought that far ahead!

The scooters were fine until you came to a hill. My mate had a few hills between his office and his home. Unlike me, he didn't have his motorcycle licence, so he immediately started that process and, within months, had bought a 250 cc Vespa. Not to be outdone, I went to Auckland Motorcycles and bought a new Triumph Bonneville America. I would have bought a Harley, but I felt that the price difference was too much; plus the Bonnie was my nod at nostalgia. Having grown up with motorbikes my whole life, it was good to start riding again.

My father not only rode motorbikes and had been a dispatch rider in World War II, but, as a teen, he had been a stuntman for Pinewood Studios in England. He had performed some incredible feats, including the gravity-defying Wall of Death, which involved riding around the vertical walls of a large wooden cylinder.

My earliest recollection of riding was being on an old Norton, which my father would ride into town with my totally blind mother sitting on the back and me standing between them, with my hands on my father's shoulders. Helmets were not compulsory in those days, so we would only wear leather flying hats (like Snoopy) to keep our ears warm.

Later, my parents bought a brand new BSA Golden Flash, with a shiny black side car, from McIvor and Veitch in Dunedin; we holidayed all over the South Island on that bike.

I can remember my father blowing the windscreen in at 91 mph (146 kph) on our way to Picton one year. I can also recall my mother riding the bike from the shop around the corner to home. My father would ride pillion and direct my mother by moving her elbows. I guess people could be forgiven for questioning my mother's blindness. I have a recollection of being about six or seven years old, and my father doing the same with me in the vacant back section behind our state house. Suddenly, he accidentally slipped off the back and dragged me with him, but because I had such a firm grip of the throttle, I opened it up as I slid backwards, launching the bike onto the top of a neighbour's hedge!

Over fifty years later, in 2012, I was speaking with Bill Veitch, the Harley dealer in Dunedin, who was aged somewhere between my parents and me. He remembered my parents well, and also me as a little kid. He told me how, a few years prior, he had come across our old sidecar behind a barn in Wanaka, but when he went back to buy it, it had gone.

JC and I decided to bypass Taupo and stop at the Licorice Café, just north of Turangi.

While riding around the shoreline of the lake, we passed some modest motel units, and I remembered staying there on a fishing trip with my good friend – the other, though vastly different, JC – John Clough. He had been thirty years old then, and I had been forty. We had some great times. One day, we decided to go fishing on Lake Taupo, so we hired a little outboard runabout and were going to trawl for trout.

Unfortunately, the weather closed in on us and we had two days of rain, which resulted in us spending our time in one of Taupo's drinking establishments. After several hours, and several beers, boredom was setting in and John said, 'Pete, why don't you dye your grey hair black?' To cut another shaggy-dog story short, I finally agreed. I questioned (possibly slurring my words) where we would get hair dye from. John said, 'I don't know, but the barmaid will know.' He asked her and she suggested the pharmacy around the corner; so we made our purchase and drove slowly back to the motel.

We had had quite a lot to drink, but John set up the bathroom with a chair in front of the mirror, then sat me down, wrapped a towel around my neck and even gave me a women's magazine to read! He proceeded to follow the instructions, and soon my head was engulfed in black foam. After twenty minutes, he instructed me to close my mouth so he could apply the solution onto the moustache I sported at the time. The realisation of what we were doing prompted a burst of spontaneous laughter, and I inadvertently sprayed the black dye solution that was on my lips all over the cream-coloured wall. We only made matters worse by trying to rub the splatters off!

I quickly wiped the foam away from my hair and moustache, and glanced in the mirror to find that John, in his intoxicated state, had not only blackened my hair, but most of my face as well! In a sobering panic, I jumped out of the chair, then into the shower and proceeded to scrub my head with all my might – all to John's protests of, 'Don't scrub it *all* off!' Needless to say, the rest of the evening, as well as the early hours of the morning, were spent cleaning up the bathroom.

The next day, we were due to go home from our failed

fishing adventure. In the morning, I awoke and looked out the window – it was a perfect day. John was asleep and I was really too exhausted to go fishing, so I quietly went back to bed without waking him. An hour or so later, John woke and said, 'Open the curtains.' Predictably, when he saw how good the weather was, it was action stations. He leaped out of bed in a flap and began making preparations for us to get out on the water. 'Damn,' I thought.

Anyway, we went out on the lake. We only had an hour before we needed to check out of our motel and, on the second trawl, I caught our only fish – a 4 lb rainbow trout. That's all John wanted. We headed back for shore, where he filleted the fish and baked it – all inside the hour. We enjoyed that breakfast and we still laugh about our experience to this day. They were good times with John.

Chapter 5

Life isn't always fair, but life is life.
It deals with us all indiscriminately,
Just as the rain falls equally on both the flowers and the weeds.
We need to shun our anxieties and fears and embrace opportunities.
We need to let the wind of change flow through our hair and live our lives
now while we are living... with confidence, commitment,
courage and with faith in God and ourselves.

The day was pleasant enough, but it hadn't decided weather-wise what it was going to do. It was overcast, but warm.

At the Licorice Café, I brought up the subject of the oceans and deserts, and JC explained that, originally, land had occupied over 70 percent of the world. This had changed after the Flood, as vast amounts of water that had sprung up from below the earth and fallen as rain to form a giant ocean now receded, leaving behind deserts and other landscapes. All that water, which had not been present on the surface of the earth prior to the Flood, had to go somewhere, and a large amount pooled into new oceans. So now the ratio of land to water was reversed.

He said that if you follow Genesis, you will learn that God made the Earth in seven days (it is believed by some that God's day equals a thousand years), and that the world was perfect, along with its inhabitants, Adam and Eve. The Garden of Eden had a perfect ecosystem because it sat on a huge water table and, in the evening, a mist would come down to assist with the optimal growth and fertility of the many plants that gave life to the numerous species of the time. All creatures were herbivores.

I interrupted and said, 'What about the dinosaurs?'

He said, 'I know what you're thinking, but their large jaws and talons were originally designed to uproot plants and trees for food, as well as to tear vegetation. There was plenty of food for every living thing.'

'So...' I said, 'I guess the fall of man really mucked all this up. Right?'

'Correct,' he said. 'When Adam and Eve were tempted and disobeyed God, it was all downhill from there.'

I said that it appeared to be much the same today. There are consequences to wrong actions.

JC again emphasised that the consequences from wrong actions were not a punishment from God, but that the actions would certainly determine the resulting path and – should those actions be wrong – they will be out of sync with how God would want us to act. He said that we must keep in mind that God chooses to work under His own natural law – which He put in place; He cannot sin and will follow through on everything He says. For example, God told Adam and Eve that they could eat from any tree in the garden except one, adding that if they ate from the forbidden tree they would surely die. They ate. They died. That was the natural consequence of what they had done.

I thought for a minute about an article I had read some time ago, which said that even specialists and scientists are puzzled as to why our bodies deteriorate and die. The human body has the ability to heal to a point, but just falls short of complete restoration as we get older. We can trace the reason for this all the way back to Genesis.

Another thought came over me – one of great understanding, as if I was thinking pure truth. The tree of the knowledge of good and evil – maybe it was a portal into another dimension used by God to visit Earth. And used by Satan – for, as the Bible says in the Book of Job, Satan came and stood before God after visiting Earth. This was just a mind-wandering thought – an aside that captured my imagination as I pondered JC's words.

JC continued, 'After God had created this world, He gave complete dominion over everything on it to Adam and Eve. When they were tempted by Satan and ate from the tree, they effectively gave that dominion to the devil. Prior to the fall of man, everyone and everything was eternal – it was forever. But now that man had rebelled, God wanted to give us a chance to redeem ourselves – so He invented time.'

Wow... I thought, time didn't exist back then.

'Donks,' he said, 'as you know from reading your Bible, it didn't take long for that bad seed, which was sown into humankind, to corrupt future generations. It resulted in the world getting so bad that it was beyond the point of redemption by human means. This then brought about the annihilation of man and beast through the Great Flood. You see, the world had no large mountains, so when the rain fell and when God caused the water table beneath the surface to erupt, the earth was engulfed in water.

'In Genesis, chapter 7, verses 11 and 12 it is written: "In the six hundredth year of Noah's life, on the seventeenth day of the second month – on that day all the springs of the great deep burst forth, and the floodgates of the heavens were opened. And rain fell on the earth forty days and forty nights."'

While JC was talking, I was tracking this through my electronic Bible on my laptop (my conversation with JC happened a few years ago, and iPads hadn't been invented yet).

'Okay,' I said, 'how did the waters recede?'

JC explained that this wasn't difficult, because God had already caused the tectonic plates to shift once, causing the water table to spill over by raising the ground below, in what we call an earthquake. So, with another shift, God again separated the tectonic plates, producing huge chasms all over the earth, and the water fell into its new settling points and pooled as oceans and lakes. That enormous movement of water is what carved the huge mountains and peaks that we now have, and why fish fossils are found on mountains and hills, and in deserts. What resulted were two continents – both of which eventually broke up. The southern one was Gondwanaland.

I thought more about this – how New Zealand had broken away from Australia; our Ozzie cousins had come away from Asia, and Asia had moved from Africa.

JC went on to say that the Great Flood and its aftermath changed the ecosystem in the world to a seasonal climate in a lot of areas. The Sahara Desert was an ocean bottom during the Flood, therefore countless marine species like plankton were deposited there to become today's oil deposits – the Middle East being the richest area for crude oil.

'Just on that,' I said, 'will we ever run out of oil?'

'No,' he said, 'there is still plenty of oil beneath the ocean, but it is more expensive to extract, and the world system, working the way that it does, will have to use up its current, more accessible – and cheaper – oil beds first. And, of course, the other complication is that the oil price directly affects the cost of food. Man's system is a little messy and it doesn't have to be this way,' he said sighing. 'This world is caught in a timeline rut.'

I thought, as he said this, that no one really understands the world money system anyway – even though they might say they do. I've always thought that the whole thing is just one big Ponzi scheme – a house of cards, a huge corporatised multilevel marketing plan. When a country goes broke, the money men can't repossess it – they just print more currency at the most convenient time to ensure the least amount of devaluation – otherwise the world system fails. We don't live in countries any more – we live in corporations. Our health and education systems are becoming increasingly corporatised. I have often felt resigned to this situation – it is what it is – we just have to live within it and make it work for us the best we can. I didn't say this out loud, but JC seemed to allow me this silent thought time and didn't comment.

'But let's not get off our original subject,' he said. 'A good example of how the waters subsided are the huge river beds with small amounts of water in them. Erosion only accounts for a tiny fraction of this phenomenon, as the world is not nearly as old as some so-called experts claim. Take the Monterey Canyon off the California coast. It's larger than the Grand Canyon, but it wasn't caused by erosion as it's under the water.'

'So…' I said, 'the Grand Canyon was formed instantly by the movement of massive flood waters, not by erosion?'

'Correct,' he said.

'Okay,' I said, 'what about the animals? How did they fit onto Noah's ark? And, how come they didn't kill one another?'

JC replied, 'The answer to your first question is that the ark was built to specific dimensions, as stated in Genesis 6:15-16. God told Noah, "This is how you are to build it: The ark is to be three hundred cubits (138 metres) long, fifty cubits (23 metres) wide and thirty cubits (13.8 metres) high. Make a roof for it, leaving below the roof an opening one cubit (46 centimetres) high all around. Put a door in the side of the ark and make lower, middle and upper decks." The craft was perfect for the task because God designed it.

'The answer to your second question is that the animals weren't carnivores at this stage – they were all herbivores, so teeth and talons were only used to forage for and strip vegetation. However, as they dispersed throughout the newly-emerged land, vegetation was initially scarce, mountains and peaks weren't accessible, water covered over 70 percent of the land, the ecosystem was altered, and deserts appeared. So hunger led to extinctions and also a change in the behaviour of certain species. Some species died out, whilst others became prey to larger species, which now, through necessity, became carnivores. However, as suitable quarry declined in numbers, so did the predators – leading to further extinctions.

'Even in later times, New Zealand was home to the largest eagle in the world and the largest flightless bird, the moa. The heavy moa would often become bogged down in swamps and become easy prey for the eagle.'

I remembered reading that quantities of moa skeletons had been found in a dried-out swamp minus their skulls. So I thought how that made sense – the eagles had carried away the moas' heads. Once the eagles' food source had become scarce, the eagles, like the moa, also became extinct. There is also the example of the dinosaurs. Throughout the world, the only ones to have survived to the present day are lizard species considerably smaller than T-Rex. So, JC's words were not that hard to comprehend.

He went on to say that the world has been obsessed with evolution and tries very hard to make it fit into history. However, that obsession is now changing in some areas of science to an 'intelligent design theory' – which is closer to the truth. But even within that theory there are still people who want to give credit to anything other than the God described in the Bible. God likes to be acknowledged and does not like being referred to as 'the universe' or some vague force of 'intelligent design'. It's like a man calling his wife 'woman' and her calling him 'man', or people saying to their friends and neighbours 'Hello, humans' when greeting them.

'Donks,' he said, 'it's going to rain soon, so let's take a short trip over the Desert Road to Taihape, and we'll shelter at the Brown Sugar Café.'

Keen to carry on our conversation, I said, 'The sky has cleared and it doesn't look like rain.'

He looked at me with a knowing half-smile and put his hand on my shoulder, saying, 'It'll rain.'

We gassed up in Turangi and headed south.

The road approaching the Desert Road was smooth and dry, and as we rode over the high country plains, I began to think about this great little country I live in. It has every possible geographical condition in such a compact area. We even have a desert!

I marvelled at the scenery and then my thoughts drifted back to the machine that made these excursions possible. As a young man, my nostalgia was for Triumphs, and the Triumph Bonneville that I had purchased was a terrific bike. I enjoyed it a lot, but, after a while, I got tired of rid-ing alone, as the Triumph clubs weren't all that active. I noticed that between ten and thirty Harleys would leave the Auckland Harley-Davidson dealership every Saturday afternoon – they were members of the Harley Owners Group (HOG). I thought, *I want to be part of that.*

So I sold my Trumpy to a mate and bought a 2006 Harley Softail Heritage Standard with only 4,000 km on the clock. This was another great bike and I enjoyed clocking up 40,000 kilometres of trouble-free riding; until one evening I attended a new Harley launch at the Floating Pavilion in Auckland. There, under the lights at the entrance, was a brand new 2009 Harley, painted pewter and pearl... a Softail Heritage Classic. My dream bike.

So, once again, I sold my existing bike to my mate, and bought myself that Heritage Classic. It's still the bike of my dreams, having now clocked over 160,000 trouble-free kilometres. I intend to do 500,000 kilometres on this motor. Actually, I would like to do 1,000,000 kilometres – but, at this rate, I'll be 111 years of age!

I was thinking about brands and how there are certain vehicle badges out there that never need justification – Harley is one of those.

I owned many makes of motorcycle and they were all wonderful, reliable bikes. But I have noticed that, now days, when someone asks me what I ride, all I have to say is, 'A Harley.' With other brands, it seems like people feel the need to justify their choice, saying things like, 'I ride a Suzuki Boulevard because...' or 'I couldn't see the point in paying out all that extra money on a Harley, when the Suzuki meets my needs.' They might be right, and maybe their bikes are marvellous. But, as I say, 'Harley' needs no justification.

An old biker named Grizz, whom I met at the Kaimai Cheese Factory Café in Waharoa, said to me, 'If you want to *get* there, buy a Jappa (a Japanese bike), if you want to *be* there, buy a Harley.'

JC rode close and in my mirror. I felt doubly secure having him there as I thought, *If he is God in human form, then he determines life and death anyway.* Then, I thought, *Whoa, I'm still not quite ready to buy into that possible identity for my fellow biker.*

Chapter 6

Live to ride for the rest of your life, and ride to live
for the rest of your life.

We rode down the hill into Taihape and parked our bikes outside the Brown Sugar Café. We took off our helmets and no sooner were we inside than the rain started. I looked at JC and, expressionless, he just winked at me.

I was still coffeed out from our previous stop, so I ordered eggs on toast with a side of beans, then sat outside in the covered garden area. JC sat opposite me and looked as though he was about to answer my next question before I had even asked it – which was, to say the least, kind of freaky.

I said to him, 'When we first met, you mentioned that Jesus is God in human flesh, right?'

'Right,' he said, as if he knew what was coming next.

I continued, 'I understand that God doesn't tolerate sin and this world is full of sin, and I understand why Jesus Christ walked this earth instead of God appearing in His full glory. And, I think I also understand that if you appeared to me as God, it would have blown my mind and the awesome complexity of God would be too much for me or anyone to handle.'

He responded, saying that when God created the world and everything in it, He also created natural laws, maps, systems and fail-safes to explain it in human terms. These natural laws are able to stand alone, as well as being an integral part of the divine grid. 'Again, to put it into your terminology: when Jesus Christ comes to your world, He abides by your world's natural laws. Also, bear in mind that, through the Holy Spirit, Jesus is omnipresent, not only in your world under your world's natural law, but in the heavens as well.'

'So...' I said, 'you're saying that it's possible for Jesus to be having a personal conversation with millions of other people like me at the same time?'

'Correct,' he said, 'but "millions" isn't relevant, as there is no limit.'

'So...' I said, 'the Holy Spirit. Tell me about this.'

He said, 'You should say, "tell me about Him". The Holy Spirit is a real, living being. The Holy Spirit completes the perfect Trinity, covering all God's laws to grace. He works within you, so that grace won't be seen as just a set of rules to observe, but as a living law, which is an important, strengthening part of your being. Any religion can teach laws, such as 'do this' or 'do that', but only the Holy Spirit can teach grace.

'But,' I said, 'if you were God, you could change the laws – you could change the shape of the future.'

'Correct, and God has done this at times,' he said, motioning me to read the Bible on my laptop. 'Read 2 Kings 20:1-11,' he said.

In those days Hezekiah became ill and was at the point of death. The prophet Isaiah son of Amoz went to him and said, 'This is what the Lord says: Put your house in order, because you are going to die; you will not recover.'

Hezekiah turned his face to the wall and prayed to the Lord, 'Remember, Lord, how I have walked before you faithfully and with wholehearted devotion and have done what is good in your eyes.' And Hezekiah wept bitterly.

Before Isaiah had left the middle court, the word of the Lord came to him: 'Go back and tell Hezekiah, the ruler of my people, "This is what the Lord, the God of your father David, says: I have heard your prayer and seen your tears; I will heal you. On the third day from now you will go up to the temple of the Lord. I will add fifteen years to your life. And I will deliver you and this city from the hand of the king of Assyria. I will defend this city for my sake and for the sake of my servant David."'

Then Isaiah said, 'Prepare a poultice of figs.' They did so and applied it to the boil, and he recovered.

Hezekiah had asked Isaiah, 'What will be the sign that the Lord will heal me and that I will go up to the temple of the Lord on the third day from now?'

Isaiah answered, 'This is the LORD's sign to you that the LORD will do what he has promised: Shall the shadow go forward ten steps, or shall it go back ten steps?'

'It is a simple matter for the shadow to go forward ten steps,' said Hezekiah. 'Rather, have it go back ten steps.'

Then the prophet Isaiah called on the LORD, and the LORD made the shadow go back the ten steps it had gone down on the stairway of Ahaz.

'Wow,' I said, 'I remember reading about this in a book written by Mr Harold Hill, President of the Curtis Engine Company in Baltimore, Maryland, who was apparently a consultant to the space program. The story circulated on the internet again more recently.

He wrote:

I think one of the most amazing things that God has for us today happened recently to our astronauts and space scientists at Green Belt, Maryland. They were checking the position of the sun, moon, and planets out in space, calculating where they would be 100 years and 1000 years from now. We have to know this, so that we don't send a satellite up and have it bump into something later in its orbits. We have to lay out the orbits in terms of the life of the satellite, and where the planets will be, so the whole thing will not bog down.

They ran the computer measurement back and forth over the centuries and it came to a halt. The computer stopped and put up a red signal, which meant that there was something wrong, either with the information fed into it or with the results as compared to the standards. They called in the service department to check it out and they said, 'What's wrong?'

Well, they found there is a day missing in space in elapsed time.

They scratched their heads and tore their hair.

There was no answer.

Finally, a Christian man on the team said, 'You know, one time I was in Sunday School and they talked about the sun standing still.'

While they didn't believe him, they didn't have an answer either, so they said, 'Show us'. He got a Bible and went back to the book of Joshua, where they found a pretty ridiculous statement for any one with 'common sense'.

There, they found the Lord saying to Joshua, 'Fear them not, I have delivered them into thy hand; there shall not a man of them stand before thee.' Joshua was concerned because he was surrounded by the enemy and if darkness fell they would overpower them. So, Joshua asked the Lord to make the sun stand still! That's right – 'The sun stood still and the moon stayed – and hasted not to go down about a whole day!'

The astronauts and scientists said, 'There is the missing day!'

They checked the computers, going back into the same time as when it was written, and found it was close, but not close enough.

The elapsed time that was missing back in Joshua's day was 23 hours and 20 minutes – not a whole day. They read the Bible and there it was 'about (approximately) a day'.

These little words in the Bible are important, but they were still in trouble because, if you cannot account for 40 minutes, you'll still be in trouble 1,000 years from now. Forty minutes had to be found, because it can be multiplied many times over in orbits.

As the Christian employee thought about it, he remembered somewhere in the Bible where it said the sun went BACKWARDS. The scientists told him he was out of his mind, but they got out the Book and read the words in 2 Kings: Hezekiah, on his deathbed, was visited by the prophet Isaiah who told him that he was not going to die. God agreed to heal him and Hezekiah asked for a sign as proof. Isaiah said, 'Do you want the sun to go ahead 10 degrees?' Hezekiah said, 'It is nothing for the sun to go ahead 10 degrees, but let the shadow return backward 10 degrees.'

Isaiah spoke to the Lord and the Lord brought the shadow ten degrees BACKWARD!

Ten degrees is exactly 40 minutes!

Twenty three hours and 20 minutes in Joshua, plus 40 minutes in Second Kings make the missing day in the universe! (References: Joshua 10:12,13; 2 Kings 20:9-11)

I was getting off track with my thoughts, so I never verified

Harold Hill's interpretation of events with JC. Apparently NASA has denied that any such incident occurred. But it brings up some fascinating ideas nonetheless and, at the end of the day, I don't need Hill's story to prove to me that the Bible is trustworthy. I believe in the truth of Biblical events. To me they are facts and, once they become fact and fact has a lid on it, then limitless faith is no longer required. So, whether Harold Hill's account of these events actually happened or not, I'm not reliant on his story to tell me that the Bible is true.

JC brought me back on track to Hezekiah, explaining that Hezekiah was about to die and, understandably, clung to life and cried out to God, not realising that God has something better in store for us all (Heaven). Hezekiah reminded God that he had been a good and faithful serv-ant. 'Not that God needs reminding,' JC said. It was true that Hezekiah was a good man and, although he was mis-interpreting God's ultimate reward for him, God gave him another fifteen years. It was during those fifteen years that Manasseh was born, and he was possibly the most evil king in biblical history. 'You see,' JC went on to say, 'if Hezekiah had trusted God and died at the appointed time, then Manasseh would never have been born, and God's natural laws would not have had to rewrite future developments to allow for this. Many, many people could have been spared from suffering at that time and in subsequent years.

I said, 'This is a good example of the consequences of not trusting God.'

I thought about this – about how the same thing could

happen today if someone loyal to God died at a young age. We, naturally, cling to this life because we know it to be fact – we are familiar with it, we see it and touch it. The unknown element of faith is so much harder to grasp – but that's faith. Faith requires faith, the same as fact requires fact.

'Okay,' said JC, 'let's head for Wellington.'

Donkey outside Auckland Harley-Davidson

On the road

Outside the Langford Store, Bainham, Golden Bay

Gilchrist's Oturehua Store, Otago

Coffee stop, Arrowtown

Cruising down Clyde main street

Denzil's first ride

Donkey and Denzil

Chapter 7

The Latin word for agnostic is ignoramus.

The rain had stopped and the warm breeze passing through the Manawatu dried out the roads immediately. As we rode over Vinegar Hill, I looked at the river beds with a new perspective on the inadequacy of the erosion theory for explaining how landscapes are formed, and how relatively minor the effects of erosion are when it comes to carving large-scale geological features.

I thought about how we seem obsessed with trying to prove evolution over creation, and how we trim the edges of our thinking to suit that point of view.

I watched a TV programme in which a creation researcher – an Australian named John MacKay – told of an agnostic evolutionist scientist friend of his who was using an incredibly powerful micron microscope to study the structure of a leaf. As this man dug down into the inner depths of the leaf – which possibly no human had seen before – he discovered that the leaf he was studying was of a more complex design than the advanced microscope he was studying it with.

Struck by this discovery, he set about looking for the origins of the leaf's designer – and he found God.

Approaching the intersection at Bulls, I looked in my mirror and JC wasn't with me. I thought he'd catch up soon enough, so I continued through to Sanson and headed along the Manawatu Plains towards Wellington. I buttoned off while checking my mirrors regularly, looking for JC, then, at Foxton, I stopped at a poultry farm that belonged to some friends of mine. As we chatted, I was listening out for the throaty throbbing hum of JC's Springer, but heard nothing. I continued on towards Wellington and, while passing through Levin, I felt an incredible sense of loneliness overwhelm me. The feeling was confidence-shattering and dissolved every thought I had into a sense of emptiness. I pulled over onto the side of the road and parked up at a picnic spot, where I sat down with my head in my hands, wondering what to do and how to rid myself of this feeling.

Tears began to fill my eyes and I was glad I still had my sunglasses on. Then, a warmth of peace came over me as I heard the rumbling of a familiar Harley approaching. It was JC and I was filled with relief. As he was parking up, I composed myself and said, 'What happened to you, couldn't you keep up?'

He smiled with his usual smile that displayed an all-encompassing confidence of depth, knowledge and approval. I thought, on the off-chance that he *was* the Son of God, *I'm so glad he gets my humour.*

Sitting there with JC, my thoughts strayed a little to church and how, occasionally, I found it hard conversing with some fellow Christians – my humour can often be lost on them. Some Christians can display a type of self-righteousness, and anything frivolous or humorous is vetted and diagnosed before they laugh; which puts a bit of a dampener on the all-important spontaneity of the exchange. Unless, of course, their pastor is there and he laughs – then they all laugh, but sometimes that's only because they feel they have received 'permission' from him. I thought, *If this is all true, and JC likes my sense of humour, then this is so cool being totally relaxed and enjoying the presence of God's Son.*

As if he read my thoughts, he said, 'Donks, I know your frustrations and disappointments with some Christians and some church groups. But remember, they are only human, and it's sometimes hard for people to communicate satisfactorily with other people in this world. Unfortunately, with Christians, you expect the benchmark to be set higher – and that's fine – but remember they are only people. You've worked in many large organisations over the years and you didn't find everyone easy to get along with. And more than just a few didn't get your humour.'

I thought back, remembering a time when I was visiting a church and some people were talking about the Mel Gibson movie, *The Passion of the Christ*. When asked for my opinion, I said that I tried to watch it, but found it boring with the subtitles and that it was too gory, telling them that, in fact, I didn't even watch the whole thing. They looked horrified; then, in a joking manner, I said, 'So, I don't even know how it ended!' I shouldn't have been surprised when one of the humourless Christians began to explain to me the ending of one of the most well-known stories in all of human history. Before they had finished describing the obvious, I seriously considered interrupting and saying, 'But I did enjoy the gag reel'!

JC said that we should ride on and catch the early evening ferry across Cook Strait to Picton, as that would be the smoothest sailing. He also said that once we were on board, we could discuss my feelings of loneliness and anxiety. Was it that obvious? Surely he wouldn't have just known?

We rode off and were soon through Otaki. As we passed through Waikanae, I caught a glimpse of a house I had once owned on the hill.

My thoughts went back to my criticisms of some of the Christians I had met during my life. Experience had shaped the way I trusted people, as I had been let down equally by Christians and non-Christians alike, so had come to that early decision to treat everyone merely as human beings – irrespective of their beliefs. In fact, I had a policy, when employing Christians, to vet them the same as anyone else, and concluded that Christians *are* the same as everyone else – being human first, with all the associated frailties, and being Christians second. In my view, this is still an accurate statement when it comes to my dealings in business and with money. Once we accept that, we can move on without placing any special qualities on any one group of people and, hopefully, the good in all will prevail without undue disappointment.

I am now careful not to confuse a belief with my *expectations* of that belief, as we are all different. In other words, a Christian belief doesn't necessarily equate to a Christian walk and way of life. Of course, ideally, it should – but being mere humans, we always fall short of total perfection.

Judgements are so fickle. For example, we usually judge ourselves by our good intentions. But others often judge us by our last worst act.

For a long time, I held onto first impressions; some first impressions that I experienced, I liked, some I didn't. But, as time moved on, both the good and the bad blended into the flow of my life, and now I have come to accept them all as being normal and natural. However, to see a situation as others see it for the first time, we need to think back to our first impressions so we can remind ourselves what it is like to view things from that perspective.

When discussing first impressions, I challenge people to walk to the other side of the street, to stand opposite their house, and look at their house as others see it. To you, it's home and, having battled the traffic, you are pleased to be there when you pull into your driveway after a long day. But, to see it as other people see it – which is simply as a house – you might notice that there's a number missing from the letterbox, or your child's scooter is still parked up in the flower garden, or there may be weeds growing out of your spouting. You see things that you have become used to – blind to – things that have evolved into the norm over the years, because it's your home.

So, I have learned from my first impressions of Christians that there are good and not so good, and I try to be one of the good ones. However, often I fall short.

The Old Testament in the Holy Bible illustrates this well, with its accurate account of the history of the nation of Israel, with all their ups and downs and shortcomings. These old scriptures won't make you clever, but they'll make you wise, and they have been written for everyday, ordinary people.

It was early evening when we descended down Kaiwharawhara Road through the Ngaio Gorge and onto the Hutt Road in Wellington. We were travelling against the flow of frustrated Wellingtonian commuters heading out of the city, which gave us a clear run, and the traffic only started to bank up as we approached our destination.

The exit to the Interislander ferry terminal has got to be one of the most confusing off-ramps in the country if you are not familiar with it. Many a time I've seen tourist camper vans trying to reverse down the motorway after missing it and trying to prevent having to trek all the way out to Petone in heavy traffic to turn around. We checked in, and eventually were called onto the ferry, where we stropped our bikes down and made our way upstairs to settle in for the three-and-a-half-hour cruise to Picton. These days, the standard of service on the Interislander ferries is as good as – and in most cases better – than ferry services in other countries around the world.

JC and I sat opposite each other on the starboard side by the main café. I cleared my emails as he got up and moved around the deck before settling down opposite me once more. I took this as my cue to start asking questions again.

'Okay,' I said, 'tell me about this sudden attack of anxiety and remorse I felt earlier while I was parked up south of Levin.'

He told me it was a typical feeling in this world we live in. He went on to say how powerful perceived situations are and how they can change our moods. I responded by asking him what he meant by 'perceived', as it was a real emotion that had gripped me.

'Was it?' he said. 'Then tell me what real situation it related to.'

Of course, I couldn't.

He went on to say that my imagination had triggered a chemical reaction in my brain to try and make something real out of nothing. He said our thoughts are very powerful and can determine our actions and well-being. He said that loneliness can be a huge distraction.

A little embarrassed about my lack of mental control, I asked him how he would have known this, as he would never have experienced anxiety – if he was God.

'When Jesus walked this earth in human form over two thousand years ago,' JC said, 'He took on all the emotions of man. He felt secure walking and performing miracles with His Father and Creator; but when it came to the time He was to take on all the sin of mankind, He had to do it alone. This was because, as sin came upon Jesus, the Father had to depart, for God cannot sin nor tolerate sin. A terrible loneliness came over Jesus and He had earlier cried out to God, "If there is some other way, let this suffering pass from me; but Your will be done, not mine." Jesus' human side made Him feel vulnerable. His time in the Garden of

Gethsemane, before facing crucifixion, was most distressing for Jesus, as God began to depart and He was starting to feel defenceless and abandoned.'

> They went to a place called Gethsemane, and Jesus said to his disciples, 'Sit here while I pray.' He took Peter, James and John along with him, and he began to be deeply distressed and troubled. 'My soul is overwhelmed with sorrow to the point of death,' he said to them. 'Stay here and keep watch.'
>
> Going a little farther, he fell to the ground and prayed that if possible the hour might pass from him. 'Father,' he said, 'everything is possible for you. Take this cup from me. Yet not what I will, but what you will.' (Mark 14:32-36)

It must have been a terrible experience for Jesus. For Him, because He knew the path that lay ahead of Him, it must have been a bit like watching a movie you have seen before, but still find yourself emotionally absorbed in, even though you already know the outcome. I felt bad, thinking how this analogy was the only one I could come up with, and how lame it seemed, considering the magnitude of the real life event. I was, however, consoled by knowing that – without doubt – Jesus is aware of what we all go through in our everyday lives.

I thought about it, and I guess we all experience what I would rate as 'Grade A hurts'. They vary, depending on the circumstances and the individual, but a Grade A hurt is a Grade A hurt. It doesn't get any worse. How do you compare the loss of a child to the breakdown of a marriage? You can't, it's personal. I thought about the pain a teenager suffers when their first boyfriend or girlfriend dumps them. We can easily brush it off, saying they're too young, and that they have their whole life ahead of them but, to them, it's as bad as it gets. It's a Grade A hurt. I recalled the emotions I felt when my first school girlfriend ignored me and the hurt I felt at the breakdown of my first marriage. The circumstances surrounding my marriage were more severe, because my two sons were involved and a substantial property was at risk, however, the level of hurt in both cases was very similar.

JC went on to say that when God departed completely (because all the sin in the world from the past to the present and into the future, for every single person that ever was, ever is and ever will be, came down upon Jesus), the pain was so great, that it killed Jesus' human body almost instantly.

I thought about the fact that crucifixion was usually a long, torturous death, and how Jesus Christ dying so suddenly was not normal. I also know that human emotional pain can be so intense that we just want to die. I know that many poor people have gone as far as to take their own lives. 'So…' I said, 'why do we have to endure all this hurt and these trials? Are they some sort of training or test?'

He reminded me of our earlier conversation about the fall of man. How God gave this, then perfect, world to Adam and how Adam took it in his own hands to disobey God and partner with Satan in sin.

I asked why God just didn't take it back. JC reminded me again that God honours His own natural laws and gave us the freewill to choose. If God had intervened then, He would have disrupted His natural laws; plus mankind would have always wondered if Satan's system would have worked.

JC continued, 'This is the fallen world you are living in now. It does function to a degree, but has a lot of faults. For example, good things happen to bad people, and bad things happen to good people – it's completely random. Not to mention all the tragedies of sickness with babies and young people dying. That decision of Adam's started a whole chain of events. Of course, God could stop it, but He wants to save as many people as He can by them making the right choice with their own freewill. Satan, on the other hand, is trying his hardest to confuse people; he knows he is doomed, but the longer he can deceive people, the longer he is delaying his ultimate demise.' JC also went on to say how God knows that death is not the end.

I thought about this and realised this world is full of dysfunctional relationships and families. Even in a so-called 'normal' family these days, a mother may have to go to work to earn money to buy appliances for the home that make chores quicker and easier, so that she has more time to go to work to earn money to buy time-saving gadgets to save time, so that she can go to work and earn more money to buy more. For some, affording appliances doesn't even come into it – it's just a battle to survive. Then, of course, there is the tragedy of babies and young people being born into a sinful world. Although the victims are usually sinless, they often have to suffer the effects of sin from a very young age. This world has a lot of faults.

JC and I decided to eat as I was becoming hungry.

Chapter 8

There is a popular saying that life is not a dress rehearsal,
that it's the real thing. I believe that this life is a dress rehearsal
and that Heaven is the real thing and the main event.

After our meal, JC and I relaxed where we were and I asked straight out, 'So… Satan is real?'

'Unfortunately, yes,' said JC, before continuing on.

'Donks, mate, you've read the Bible. Lucifer was an angel of authority in Heaven, but got a little too big for his boots, so to speak, and revolted against God. After being defeated, Lucifer's name was changed to Satan.

'He had a system which he deemed better than God's and convinced one third of the angels to go with him. He was defeated, along with his followers, and cast out of Heaven, and this is the system you are living within today. It almost works, but it's full of flaws.

'You see, Donks,' he said, 'God could have squashed it there and then, but Satan had convinced a third of the angels that his system was better. So, God let Satan's plan play out in this world of ours with all its sadness and hurts.

There are good times, but not perfect times, and – of course – God wants us to live in a perfect world. Satan has lost the battle and is going down big time, and wants to drag as many of us down with him as he can. Isn't that also a bad trait that we sometimes see in human nature?'

'Good God,' I said jokingly, 'sounds like the plot of some kind of fantasy sci-fi movie. Did God write the plot for *Star Wars*?'

JC laughed and said, 'Of course! *Star Wars* and many other movies are based on a universal and biblical theme of a war in Heaven between good and evil.'

He went on to say that when Satan was cast out, he travelled back and forth from Heaven to Earth (as illustrated in the book of Job). Because God gave all dominion and authority over the Earth to Adam, when Adam gave in to temptation, he effectively gave a measure of that power to Satan. So, God living and abiding by His own natural laws, will only enter into and change our lives by our invitation. He gave us freewill and honours that. Of course, He could intervene (and does occasionally carefully intervene through miracles), but just imagine the possibly dire consequences of God breaking His natural laws. Worst case scenario, the whole universe would collapse.

JC also explained that our spirit is housed in an organic body and that our spirit doesn't die.

I agreed with this and said, 'It's my understanding that it's the same elements and nutrients that make up our body that are found in the ground, such as iron and calcium, etc. So, when this 'organic dwelling' gives up and dies, our spirit has to go somewhere. I guess I want mine to go to the right place. I believe we have a choice.'

'That's the one, Donks,' he said, as he winked with acknowledgement.

That threw me out a bit. The whole situation was still messing with my mind. Was I experiencing the Son of God – who is God in human form – being a regular bloke and winking at me in acknowledgement? I had to check myself, because I still wasn't ready to buy into the possibility that this was JC's true identity, and I wanted to keep things – as I thought at the time – 'real'.

However, there was no doubt I was gaining a lot of respect for JC's knowledge and wisdom, so I continued to put my reservations aside. The conversation was on a roll and we were talking about the really important things in life. I thought about the popular saying that life is not a dress rehearsal, that it's the real thing and that there is nothing afterwards, so we have to get it right. Whereas, I believe life *is* a dress rehearsal and that Heaven is the main event. I believe, like all dress rehearsals, it is just the final run-through before the real thing; so it is important to try and get it right, but if you get it wrong, you can put it right, because the final audience (Heaven) isn't there yet. 'So…' I said out loud, 'I guess we can step out there and take a few risks and really live this life?'

JC smiled, as if he knew what I was going to say and when I was going to say it.

I put it straight to JC that I was sick and tired of all the crap that had been handed down to me over the years, and that if God was who JC said He was, then why didn't He shield me?

He said that I make my own decisions, and some are right and some are wrong – sometimes it was those decisions that led to crap. They are *my* decisions and I must deal with the outcome of my choices. 'But,' he said, 'no matter the cause of the crap – whether you are in some way responsible or not – Jesus is always here to help.' He carried on, saying that maybe Jesus had stepped in on 73 occasions when my life was in danger, but that I was never aware of it. He said this with an expression of knowing.

I was again taken aback by this information and I reacted, lashing out a little, telling him I was tired of being caught up in the middle of this cosmic war of God versus Satan, and asking why couldn't God just sort it out without involving me.

Again, he reminded me that God had given this world to Adam and that Adam had inadvertently given Satan a greater level of influence, clarifying once more that as long as Satan has a level of dominion in our world, God's representation here will generally only occur by our invitation.

After the original sin of man, God introduced death. Not as a punishment for man, but to end man's future torment of living in a fallen world, of having to sit back and watch hopelessly while future generations made it worse, of knowing there was nothing we could do. Death is for our release, so that we can start again. God gave us a reset button.

JC continued to explain that Satan has been defeated

and knows this, but because God – ideally – wants every-one to be saved by giving their life over to Jesus, God is delaying the destruction of this world, until everyone has had the opportunity to be redeemed. Satan is working very hard to delay this in order to keep his own life going as long as possible and is using temptation to draw people away from God. God is the only One who knows the date of the end of time. But, in the scale of things, it will be sooner rather than later.

In the scale of things? I thought. *That doesn't tell me much. In the scale of things, our life on this earth is extremely short.* Then I thought, *Unless you're in a queue at the post office or waiting for the toast to pop up.*

The ferry soon docked in Picton and we decided to stay the night, as it was getting late.

The next day, we rode off towards Queen Charlotte Sound. The day was stunning, and I found the twists and turns therapeutic as I interacted with the road and cleared my mind. We exited at Havelock and headed for the perfect riding hills of the Rai Saddle and its neighbour, Whangamoa.

Memories of my childhood summer holidays came flood-ing back as we rode through Canvastown, then passed the Trout Hotel and the pretty little stopover point of Pelorus Bridge. We were soon riding through Nelson, heading for Motueka and Kaiteriteri Beach. My parents had lived in this area for twenty years after retiring from Dunedin many years ago, building a house in Brooklyn by the Motueka River and having a good life there with the many friends they made. My father drove a little blue 1969 Mitsubishi

Colt, which was their pride and joy and I still have that car today. I drive it regularly as I've never had the heart to sell it, and it has come in handy as a second vehicle.

We parted company briefly in Nelson as I called in to see my very good friends, Lloyd and Gwen Ewing, who own a business just out of Richmond; I had a good catch up with them as usual.

Naturally, I knew my way down the West Bank Road. We crossed the pure fresh water of the Motueka River at the last bridge and rode straight through Tapawera (like most people seem to do), joined SH6 (the Kohatu-Kawatiri Highway) and rode through the relatively unknown, but peaceful and private, campsite of Quinney's Bush. SH6 then morphed into the Kawatiri-Murchison Highway and, after tracking the Buller River, we stopped for a well-deserved break and lunch at Murchison.

When we carried on, there were no cars on the road, so it puzzled me why there were so many passing lanes. That, to me, is the most frustrating thing about riding the South Island – there are passing lanes but no one to pass… I just wish they would save them all up and give them to the North Island! We turned off onto the Upper Buller Gorge Road at the entrance of the Shenandoah Highway, and headed west for the historic town of Inangahua – a place that made the headlines in 1968 when an earthquake resulted in 70 percent of the town being made uninhabitable.

We chose SH67 and headed towards the West Coast town of Westport – the home of the Good Bastards Micro Brewery (which was well worth a visit, but I chose not to take JC there). After gassing up, we were going to head along the scenic route to Greymouth, taking in the old coal mining town of Denniston, and the natural wonder of the Pancake Rocks. However, JC decided to head elsewhere, so we agreed to meet up the next day at Lake Brunner. I hadn't banked on the weather closing in so rapidly. I decided to gap it and ride straight to Blackball to find accommodation at the infamous pub, Formerly The Blackball Hilton.

Blackball was established around 1893 by the transit gold miners on their way to making their fortune. Later, with the establishment of coal mines in the area, Blackball made the headlines with the 1908 Crib Time strike. According to a newspaper clipping on the wall of the pub, the miners were fined in court for breaking the law over wanting their lunch break extended from fifteen minutes to thirty minutes, and – ironically – the judge adjourned the court for eighty minutes for lunch. During the coal mining boom, the population peaked at 1,200, but is currently 330 (give or take a sheep or two).

The pub itself was founded in 1910 as the Dominion Hotel, and later renamed after the mine manager and the main street (Hilton Street). However, Paris's dad took exception to the name 'The Blackball Hilton' and, after many letters and the threat of law suits, the name was changed to 'Formerly The Blackball Hilton'.

The Hilton offers a variety of budget accommodation options and is a bikers' heaven. The rooms are upstairs, with either a double bed or twin singles, and there is one large dormitory with eight beds. The cost per room was $55 per night and who would complain about that? The rooms don't have facilities, but it's only a short, creaky wander down the hallway to poop and shower. The meals are generous and the breakfast will set you up until the following evening.

Making myself at home, I was able to dry out my gear in front of the roaring fire in the lounge area that evening.

The downside of Blackball – or maybe it's an upside – was that Vodafone hadn't yet made it to this little West Coast town – so to get any cell phone coverage, you had to stand in the main street on the centre line. This was a nuisance but quite safe, even during peak hour traffic, which averages one car every fifteen minutes – usually an old Austin Ute or Hillman Minx.

The next day, the rain cleared and the sun came out, and eight Auckland HOG Chapter members arrived at the hotel, one of which was Krash and his wife, Carmel.

After settling in, Krash came and sat at the table out front as I was loading my bike in the pleasant warmth of the morning sun. The peace was broken by a local farmer moving his flock of sheep down the main street in front of us. The sun was intense early that day, and the sheep were panting with their tongues hanging out. It was then that Krash embarrassed himself by saying, 'Wow, those sheep are hot.' I took this opportunity to disown Krash, gear up and ride out!

Chapter 9

'God owns everything. We don't own anything, we are just stewards
of what God owns; if you think you own anything,
then try taking it with you when you die.' – Peter Mortlock

I met up with JC at a café in Moana and, as we settled down overlooking the Moana Railway Station, I asked him about another subject that had been on my mind – tithing. He said that, in this world, tithing can be an enormous blessing or an enormous barrier.

Tithing – the giving of ten percent of your income – was introduced as a discipline for God's people. JC went on to say that God doesn't need our money – but His people and His Church do, so that they can function in this world. God also made a promise that you can test Him on. When you give, you will receive back tenfold, 'pressed down and overflowing'.

Give, and it will be given to you. A good measure, pressed down, shaken together and running over, will be poured into your lap. For the measure you use, it will be measured to you. (Luke 6:38)

I noticed a common thread in the Old Testament. Even during occupation by other nations, God's obedient people flourished. When I was growing up, I remember hearing that the Jewish people in the United States made up 10 percent of the population, but it was estimated they controlled 80 percent of the wealth. Even today, the Jewish people and those obedient to God prosper in all areas. You only have to look at the Hollywood Oscars and other entertainment awards.

I asked JC about people who couldn't afford to tithe. He replied that 10 percent is 10 percent. He said tithing is not an amount or a condition for God's love or your wellbeing – His grace through His Son provides this. Rather, tithing is your discipline – for your benefit and the benefit of His Church.

I asked if we could tithe our time.

'Yes, of course,' he said, 'but tithe in money as well if you want God's promise to receive back tenfold, pressed down and overflowing.' He went on to say that however you give, and whatever you give, will be the measure in which you receive. Tithing doesn't have to be in one area – it can be in lots of ways at once – and the increased measure will be given back to you in those many ways.

He turned and said to me, 'Donks, you are a great tither of money, you are a generous man.' My eyes began to water; that acknowledgement had an immense meaning and such satisfaction I cannot put into words. I felt so good about myself, it was such an unbelievable feeling. It was an honour to be considered a generous man.

I said to JC that it was my understanding that we can test God on this promise, and JC said that this was correct. I said also that I understood that we cannot 'out-give' God – that it is impossible to give more than God will give us. He said that this also was correct. Then I said, 'Then how come, more often than not, I feel as if I am out-giving God?'

JC laughed and said, 'When you expect a reward, you limit your direction of expectation. Sometimes the best reward is not what you expect – God often over-delivers. Sometimes we are waiting for what we think we deserve, and can come close to missing something far greater that God is doing or has already done for us.'

I thought about that and thought how true it was.

He asked if I had ever run out of money, and I said, 'No, but I've come close.' He said that God will always provide. I told him that was fine, but what about the 'tenfold, pressed down and overflowing'? He said that this is where faith and expectation come in.

'Donks,' he said, 'you don't fully understand that yet.'

'But, how come it seems to work with other people?' I asked.

'People are all individuals and different. That's why one person's tenfold, pressed down and overflowing can be greater than another's. Test God on this,' he said.

'I thought I was,' I murmured under my breath. I felt straight away that he had heard me, but he didn't flinch and I felt a little like a spoiled brat.

He went on to say that tithing is like sowing a seed. You can't just plough dirt and expect a harvest. You need to plant the seed. If you wanted to grow something, and you just ploughed the ground and left it, you wouldn't get a harvest. You could yell at the ground and stomp your feet in frustration. Seeing your predicament, someone might come along and ask if you had planted any seed. Perhaps you would reply that you hadn't, because you wanted to keep your seed to eat. Well, if you were a farmer, you would know that you must put aside a certain amount of grain to sow for next season's harvest. The same principle applies with giving. Giving is sowing, and sowing reaps a harvest.

The principle of sowing and reaping, means that first you have to give. Whatever you give God as an offering, He will multiply by ten times. So, if you give Him nothing, He will multiply that by ten times. Ten times zero is zero.

In the Bible, the Gospels tell the story of how Jesus fed thousands of people with just a few loaves of bread and some fish (Matthew 14:13-21 and 15:32-16:10, Mark 6:31-44 and 8:1-9, Luke 9:10-17, and John 6:5-15). When Jesus fed the five thousand with five loaves and two fish, He blessed the bread and fish, then told the disciples to distribute it. It was at that giving-out point that it multiplied and never ran out. Basketfuls of leftovers were picked up afterwards. (There is some discrepancy in the Gospels about the numbers of people who were fed in this well-witnessed account – it was either 5,000 or 4,000. This is because, in those days, they only counted the male adults at such events, however we can assume there were also many women and children gathered there, and so the numbers are something of an approximation.)

As long as the earth endures, seedtime and harvest, cold and heat, summer and winter, day and night will never cease. (Genesis 8:22)

Now, when you go to the New Testament, 2 Corinthians 9:10-11, you can then define what seed can mean.

Now he (God) who supplies seed to the sower and bread for food will also supply and increase your store of seed and will enlarge the harvest of your righteousness. You will be enriched in every way so that you can be generous on every occasion, and through us your generosity will result in thanksgiving to God. (2 Corinthians 9:10,11)

Seed can mean many things to many people.
It's not easy for people to give in faith – the Psalmist struggled the same way we do with natural apprehension.

Those who go out weeping, carrying seed to sow, will return with songs of joy, carrying sheaves with them. (Psalm 126:6)

'Donks, your dreams are waiting to be financed by your own faith. Just plant your seed and wait for the harvest of your generosity. From one apple comes many seeds.'
He paused for a while and then looked at me closely. 'Donks, what verse is that tattooed on you arm?'
'Hebrews 10:35-36,' I said.
Knowingly, he asked me why I had it tattooed on my arm.

I cheekily suggested that he should know why. I explained how those verses from the Bible had helped me through some of my lowest and loneliest times. He then said that maybe I should cease using it only as a backstop, and start using it every day to give me the confidence to make right choices and better decisions.

> So do not throw away your confidence; it will be richly rewarded. You need to persevere so that when you have done the will of God, you will receive what he has promised. (Hebrews 10:35-36)

A number of years ago, a man named Dan Andrews, who was a pastor in Waiuku, had given me those verses as part of a prophecy. JC asked if I remembered Dan speaking those words, and now reminded me that this promise was from God and is never ending. I could live this promise now, tomorrow and forever. Then it twigged – how did he know Dan Andrews had given me those verses? When I asked him, he just smiled.

'Now, I will reinforce it with this promise...' said JC.

> And I will do whatever you ask in my name, so that the Father may be glorified in the Son. (John 14:13)

I felt extremely confident after hearing these words. 'I feel like I could walk on water!'

JC laughed out loud and gave me an acknowledging shove.

I thought for a moment. 'But why do these feelings never seem to last? Even in the Bible there appears to be a pattern – big miracles happen, but people still struggle with their confidence.'

'Faith is work in progress, otherwise it wouldn't be faith,' said JC. 'Remember now, as Hebrews 11:1 explains, faith is being sure of what we hope for and being convinced of what we do not see. If it wasn't a work in progress, it would be fact, and – as you know – fact ends faith. When you have faith that something will happen and it does – maybe for healing and you are healed – you don't require faith any more, because it's now fact. When fact is in place, it has a limiting effect and you often cannot go beyond that point – whereas faith has no boundaries.'

He again made the powerful statement that *fact ends faith*. 'In many circumstances this reality is fine, and this is how we reap our reward when applying faith – we see what we once had faith for, turn into something concrete,' he explained. 'But, fact can be assessed and we can analyse it and critique it, and in some cases, when faith becomes fact, faith ends prematurely. Instead, faith should be unlimited and keep on going. When we experience the reward of faith, rather than switching faith off, we should gain even greater faith.'

JC then suggested we push on through Arthur's Pass, as it was such a fine, clear day.

Each of New Zealand's South Island mountain passes has its own natural and unique beauty. The West Coast side of the Lewis Pass would be the most beautiful, while

Arthur's Pass is breathtaking, especially riding from west to east, toward Death's Elbow. The Haast Pass would come in at number three in my ranking, with the Lindis Pass being the plainest, but still well worth the ride.

The little-known Danseys Pass, between Central Otago and North Otago, is one out of the box. It's not a practical pass for most Harley riders, but to travel from the Livingstone end to Naseby offers some nice surprises. The road from north to south is very narrow and is coated in rough gravel. It is often closed due to snow in the winter. But, along this rugged, dusty track, you come across the revamped Danseys Pass Coach Inn on the top of a hill, in the middle of nowhere. You are forced to slow down as the publican places his outdoor furniture in the centre of the road to slow traffic and keep the dust down. The inn, originally built in 1862, has excellent accommodation and is well worth a night's stay.

JC and I rode upwards, into the stunning majesty of Arthur's Pass, roaring through the semi-deserted town of Otira. I can remember stopping here numerous times with my mate, Duds, and us two smiling at each other as we observed the elderly owners sitting out on the old deck of the hotel, having to reluctantly break their routine by getting up to serve us.

JC and I continued on, riding over and under the concrete structures that now give the pass its stability, then stopped at the top to observe the route we had travelled. Kea, a native New Zealand parrot, were abundant and predictably nosy. I remember that the last time I was there, one actually tore a hole in my mate Hogster's motorbike seat – not an uncommon occurrence in that scenic area. We continued over Arthur's, and, with a warm north-west wind behind us, we rode down into the vast Canterbury Plains, stopping in Oxford at Seagars for a coffee and some of Jo Seagar's fine food.

We then headed to Geraldine for the night.

JC disappeared for the rest of the evening. So, after a home-cooked meal at the Geraldine Heritage Hotel, I retired and drifted into a sound sleep.

Chapter 10

Live life while you are living.

In the morning, after breakfast, JC was already at his bike waiting for me. We left Geraldine on a bright crisp summer's morning and rode on towards Lake Tekapo. Although the breeze generated by my momentum was cool, the sun was hot, and you sure noticed the difference when you rode through shaded areas. We approached Tekapo and stopped for a coffee.

I asked JC how he rates sin. He told me he didn't. He said that most of this world sees sin as an action of wrong, with varying degrees of severity. He said sin is separation from God, and sin is sin. This world turned to sin with the fall of man. So, being born into this world, you were born separated from God through no direct fault of yours. However, the same way Adam invited Satan's involvement in the way this world operates, you can invite God into your world because you have the freewill to do so.

I decided to put it straight out there and asked him about homosexuality. He said that, with no question of doubt, this is a sin. I pointed out that this is not a popular stance in today's world. He said that, just because something is popular, doesn't make it right. I asked him how he felt about gay people.

'I feel the same way about them as I feel about you and about everyone else in the world – good or bad. Dishonest people, honest people, adulterous people, thieves and murderers. I hate the sin, but I love the sinner,' he said.

'But,' I asked, 'how can you place, let's say, an honest, kind, gay person in the same sin camp as a murderer?'

'Sin is separation from God and not an action. I'm not as concerned about how you rate a person's wrongdoing as I am about you being separated from God. If you weren't separated from God, then you wouldn't sin. This world has deteriorated in every way because of sin. We spoke at the start of our journey about how sin was the cause of the disintegration of the perfect ecosystem that was designed for this world. Sin is the cause of all our physical and mental discrepancies and diseases.'

I thought about the make-up of men and women, and of the vast similarities in our bodies, other than the main difference – the Y and X chromosome. I considered how the parallels make sense – for, as Genesis shows, God shaped woman from man. The original genetic design was amazing. Then sin entered and separated us from God, and deterioration set in.

I remember reading somewhere that a group of psychiatrists had done research on a group of subjects. They researched why Person A could drink alcohol and not become an alcoholic, yet when Person B drank alcohol, alcoholism took hold. It appears that we are born with various tendencies that aren't active until triggered – the catalyst in this case being alcohol. They concluded that the same condition was apparent regarding homosexuality – that the tendency was stronger in some individuals than in others and, once sparked by action, the tendency could gain a foothold. I believe Satan understands this, and this is why he promotes all kinds of sinful actions, through the media, through advertising, and even through our education system, to confuse already-inquisitive and confused youth. They are a major target of Satan and, in our politically-correct world, we are going along with it.

So, in summary, my understanding is that we are all born with various predispositions – whether they be because of our genes or innate desires – and, once action is taken towards these, then they have a foothold. Some people may say that if God made us, then He put those tendencies there. I say that, in the beginning, God made humans perfect, but with the fall of man came corruption in all areas, so that sinful tendencies now drive people towards lifestyles of gambling, alcohol and sexual promiscuity – all of which are a separation from God.

I have met many men with feminine characteristics of movement and voice, and sometimes the assumption has been that these guys were gay, even though they weren't. But who knows? What would have happened if they had had that tendency and acted on it? I wonder, too, how many potential gambling addicts have crossed my path, but have never acted on it? I read an interesting article by Paul Cameron, PhD, titled, 'What Causes Homosexual Desire and Can It Be Changed?'

Please remember in reading this, that God loves us all (I'm not preaching some kind of hatred against people), and that sin is not a particular action but rather an overall separation from God.

I sometimes felt like JC might have been guiding my thoughts. Either that, or he was very patiently allowing me to drift off in silent consideration for what appeared to be long periods of time.

We were soon back on our bikes, heading past vivid blue man-made waterways and salmon farms, then through Omarama and over the Lindis Pass, stopping at Clyde for the night.

That evening, I visited the closest person I have to a big sister, Elaine, and her husband, Graeme. Elaine was an exceptional friend to my family and wrote a history of my parents, which assisted me in writing this book.

I never saw JC that night – although his bike remained parked beside mine – but I had a great sleep and met him for breakfast at my favourite café, The Bank Café. Their famous cheese rolls are the best in the world.

JC said he would meet with me at St Bathans later that evening, so we parted company and I rode on alone down through Omakau and the Maniototo. On the way, I encountered flocks of sheep and the odd herd of cattle. Livestock is always a hazard for motorcyclists, and this time was no exception. One of the herds had a massive white bull in its midst, taking up more than his fair share of the road. Fortunately, with the aid of the local cocky on his ATV, I negotiated through the throng and rode carefully past the bull. The beast himself looked reasonably docile, but his swinging testicles, as he swaggered along, took a bit of negotiating. One nudge from an unfortunately timed swing could have knocked me off my bike!

The town of St Bathans is like stepping back 200 years, and although many of its original dwellings are still intact, functioning and very much lived in, most of the mud brick houses that once clustered along its streets have since disappeared.

However, the St Bathans Hall remains and is the oldest continually used mud-brick hall in New Zealand. It was built in 1892/93 by the local publican and, across the years, has been used as a theatre, Masonic lodge, schoolroom, mining company office and dance hall. It is classified as a Category 2 Historic Place.

The Vulcan (formerly Ballarat) Hotel in St Bathans is probably one of New Zealand's most photographed hotels, and was built of mud brick back in 1882 – two decades after gold was first discovered in the region. The current publicans, Mike and Jude Cavanagh, make you feel welcome in that no-frills Central Otago kind of way for which the region is renowned. I'm not fully an Aucklander, having spent my first thirty years in the Otago region, so I'm a bit biased toward Otago, which will always be considered home to me.

There are two double rooms at the Vulcan and a few

bunk rooms with bathroom facilities down the hall. Trust me when I tell you – Jude's breakfasts will set you up for the day, and possibly the next day as well. But there's more to this establishment than beer, food and rooms. The Vulcan's ghost story is just part of the unique appeal of the place. The ghost – who was evidently a working lady of the night – is said to occupy Room One.

I remember staying there with my good friends, the Blok and the Bride. Blok, remaining true to his Polynesian superstitions, never slept a wink that night because of the ghost. However, it wasn't all bad as he didn't snore, and the Bride got her best sleep in ages – as did my favourite riding mate, Dudley, and I, who were sharing in an adjoining bunk room. As a joke, I pinned $20 on my door hoping for a visit from the apparition. But no such luck, I'm afraid – so I guess she didn't recognise modern currency.

It was just on lunchtime when I booked into the Vulcan Hotel that day, so I spent the rest of the afternoon relaxing and catching up with Mike and Jude, and other friendly locals. I decided to go for a stroll around the famous man-made lakes that evening, to help Jude's excellent lamb roast digest, because I had eaten far too much.

JC's familiar figure joined me. I had grown used to him just showing up like this, and we sat on a large log under the clear, star-studded sky of Central Otago. As usual, he seemed to be expecting my question.

'If God is omnipresent,' I said, 'and let's just say you are the Son of God, you could be having a similar personal conversation with someone else as well as me, right?'

'Yes,' he answered, 'through the Holy Spirit, and not only with someone else, but somewhere else, or even, with someone else in a different time.' He told me not to try and analyse this, as it was a law beyond my capabilities, and in my limited understanding it could disappoint me if it led me to think that our conversation wasn't exclusive and personal, when of course it was.

I asked, if he wasn't God's Son, did he make a habit of conversing with lost souls on his travels? He said there was a lady he knew, and that the two of them had been shadowing one another for many years as their paths crossed. I had no idea what or who he was talking about, but by now had learned to just go with the flow.

He told me that we were to part company that night, as he wanted to travel further south.

'You've got a Bularangi Harley-Davidson tour in Auckland on Sunday that you should get back for,' he said.

I was puzzled. 'I don't know anything about a tour this weekend,' I said.

'Kerry was down to take a paid pillion passenger, but he will change to another ride. Ali will call you on Saturday, asking you to fill the gap.'

With my friends Baz and Ali Howie, I was involved with the Bularangi Motorbikes Harley Tours and Promotions company, and often helped out with motorbike tours and chauffeuring. Kerry did the same as well as other biker friends. But I'd never chatted to JC about this.

'That's strange,' I said, 'but I'll go with it.'

Chapter 11

The way home to the future.

I was curious about the mystery woman JC had mentioned earlier, so I asked him to tell me more about her.

He smiled, and I could see he was happy about my interest. 'I won't go into too much specific detail, but I'll tell you a little bit of her story and some of the events that have shaped her life so far.'

Here's what I found out...

Her name was Denzil and she was born in Palmerston North to loving parents on the 24th of November 1949 – the same year as me. She was the youngest of three sisters, and she was fortunate to be brought up in a safe family environment.

At the age of twenty-one, in Christchurch, she gave her life over to Jesus Christ and was soon married and helping out in her church alongside her husband, who was a motorcycle mechanic. She gave birth to a son when she was twenty-five years of age and, at twenty-eight, was widowed by her husband's tragic death. This event completely turned her life upside-down, causing her to question her faith.

JC said that he wanted to help her, but she rejected any assistance from him or her church, and decided to take control of her own life and future. 'I kept in touch with her throughout her life, as I knew the future that God had in place for her,' said JC. 'Many times I would remind her about this verse from the Book of Jeremiah:

'For I know the plans I have for you,' declares the Lord, 'plans to prosper you and not to harm you, plans to give you hope and a future.' (Jeremiah 29:11)

'Unfortunately, she was focused and determined on doing things her way, which always ends up being the long way. She moved to Auckland with her son and bought a house in Ponsonby. This was the era of women's rights and independent thinking.'

I interrupted and said lightheartedly, 'When men were encouraged to switch from beer to wine, and sit around fondue sets cooking tofu?' JC didn't flinch and carried on talking, letting my attempt at humour slide by.

Denzil studied how to renovate a house, even going to the gym to build her strength. She renovated her home by whatever methods she deemed fit. 'Denzil had skills and resources to get men to do things for her – some of these men I approved of, many I didn't – and that pattern of strategies continued on,' said JC.

Denzil thought about the social environment in which

she was bringing up her son, and wondered if he would be better off living with her eldest sister and brother-in-law on their family farm in the Bay of Plenty. The boy had a fantastic upbringing on his aunty and uncle's farm, with loving guardians, pet lambs, farm bikes and sport, and grew into a fine, responsible young man – now in his forties, married and living in Munich, Germany.

I told JC that I understood where Denzil was coming from; that being left alone to fend for yourself with the added responsibility of a child (or children, in my case) was a huge undertaking. I knew that feeling and I knew what kind of thoughts would have been going through her head. When I was in that situation all those years ago, I too rationalised things into a perspective which – today – I wouldn't rate as normal.

But, there were differences between Denzil's story and mine. When I couldn't cope on my own, I knew I needed support to get me through, so I turned to God. Denzil, however, turned away from God. I guess, because I was new to God at that time, I had no prior expectations of Him, so – when things went bad for me – I had the advantage of having no past disappointments to influence my thinking. *Past performance hadn't dulled my expectation for new opportunities.*

At work, in an environment that JC said he also didn't approve of, Denzil was introduced to the manager of the German-based Opel Rally Team. She accepted a job as the team assistant during its rally tour of Brazil, organising various catered and social functions, while also taking a support role in the day-to-day running of the team. She flew to Los Angeles, then on to Brazil, where she contracted hepatitis A, through eating the local fresh food, and became very ill.

As JC related this story to me, I interrupted and asked why God had just stood back and watched as this chain of events unfolded in Denzil's life – why He hadn't intervened.

'Denzil was wandering in the wilderness, and she had rejected God,' said JC. 'Because of God's natural laws for mankind, she was free to choose and was very strong-willed. In the greater scheme, it was in her spiritual interests to play this out. From a worldly point of view, she was very capable and extremely resourceful, but God was furthermost from her mind.'

On the completion of her contract in Brazil, she returned to Los Angeles to begin exploring the world. Although LA was intended to be just a stopover on the way to Europe, she fell in love with the City of Angels, and ended up staying for nearly twenty years.

Many Americans being avid collectors, Denzil made a good living making teddy bears – not only for those who treasured them in their own personal collections, but also for designers and decorators of film sets. Living in Burbank, California, she was in the perfect place – right in the middle of the studio area of Hollywood.

She was very talented, designing and making sought-after biker bears riding Harley-Davidsons. In fact, my Springer is a life-size version of one of the models she made.

'Although she wasn't following God, I was very proud that she was using the talents He had given her,' said JC.

She was very innovative and, in her work, used cogs and chains from the instruments and innards of WWII planes – some of which dated back to the 1930s and 1940s.

One day, at the age of thirty-seven, Denzil visited the dentist. During his check-up, he became concerned about her overall health and sent her to a specialist. The specialist confirmed that she had lymphoma cancer. This came as a shock to Denzil, but she still didn't enlist God's help. Fortunately, God knew her condition was treatable. Then, ten years later, she was diagnosed with breast cancer, and – having obtained a Green Card by marrying her best friend, Nevin – she returned to New Zealand for treatment, which was successful.

JC continued, 'She still wasn't willing to ask me for help, and returned to the States, but found that, because so much time had elapsed, she couldn't get her life up and running again. Next time I caught up with her, I suggested that she return to New Zealand, and she came home to be with her much-loved Papa for his eightieth birthday celebrations.'

Denzil stayed on in New Zealand and, along with her sister, Glenda, trained and competed in marathons. She went on to complete the New York, Paris and London Marathons, as well as the Auckland Marathon (seven times) and the Rotorua Marathon (thirteen times).

Ten years after her breast cancer, Denzil collapsed and was diagnosed with a large inoperable tumour – the size of a tennis ball – on her spine. 'This threatened to take away the use of her leg, yet Denzil still didn't turn to God,' said JC. 'But I again kept in close contact with her while she received chemotherapy treatment. This shrank the tumour, but unfortunately greatly depleted her immune system, which remains fragile to this day.'

Before long, Denzil's focus and determination to get well had her out on the streets in a Zimmer frame, teaching herself to walk again. Six months after completing her chemotherapy, she walked the Auckland Half Marathon. Just six months after that, she completed another Rotorua Marathon.

'She sounds like a remarkable woman,' I said.

'All God's creations are remarkable,' JC answered.

I then said, 'And she likes Harleys! Could this be the perfect woman?' Again, JC didn't flinch, and I wondered if I had overstepped the boundary of humour.

Being more serious, I said, 'I hope that one day soon she will come to realise how you and God feel about her.'

'One day,' he said.

The following morning, JC and I parted company, but it didn't seem like a farewell or a goodbye. It certainly wasn't sad – in fact I was feeling quite inspired. JC told me that the Holy Spirit was always with me and that my strength in this understanding would grow.

I rode off down through Ranfurly, opting to ride the undulating hills to Dunedin via Middlemarch. In Dunedin, I stayed with my oldest best friend, Allan, and we had a great catch-up, as always, talking about anything and everything. But I didn't feel that the time was right to mention JC.

The next day, I called on some more great supportive friends in Waikouaiti – Jeff and Aileen Winmill, who are farmers. I ended up staying the night with them as we reflected back on past fun times. The following day I set off up SH1 for home. I couldn't remember if I'd ever ridden SH1 all the way before. I knew I'd driven it many times but, with the Harley, I'd always been inclined to zigzag across the South Island to take in all the wonderful mountain passes.

As I rounded the corner at Shag Point, about sixty kilometres north of Dunedin, I recalled the large seal colony there and how, as a child, I would fish off the rocks with my family. I remember one day struggling to throw out my fishing line. A friend of my family who seemed to know a lot about everything, grabbed my rod and reel and proceeded to show me the correct way to cast, only to have the line end up all over the place, in a tangled bird's nest of nylon. It was then that a huge sea lion stuck its head up from the rocks in front of us and, with a loud bark and prolonged clapping of its fins, appeared to show great amusement – much to the embarrassment of our family friend.

The area is riddled with huge old coal mines dating back to 1863. The main mine had a 140-metre-long main shaft, and a network of tunnels that extended out from the coastline to a depth of about eighty metres. Quite incredible, I thought, for the time – particularly in light of the workers having to deal with the problem of seawater continually seeping in. Brave men those miners.

My journey was reasonably uneventful and, strangely and wonderfully, I didn't feel alone because I had the feeling I wasn't alone.

Just past Shag Point, you arrive at the little town of Moeraki. It is best known for the Moeraki Boulders, which are unusually large, spherical rocks that lie along the shoreline on a stretch of Koekohe Beach. But Moeraki is also known to have the best seafood restaurant in the world – Fleur's Place – which I had to visit.

After Moeraki, I made excellent time and soon found myself gapping it through to Kaikoura. The going was good, so I carried on up the refreshing Kaikoura coast and stayed the night at the Kaikoura Cottage Motels in Mill Road. Aileen and Jeff had recommended the place, and they had not only made a booking for me but paid the night's accommodation as well. This wasn't the first time I had been a recipient of Jeff and Aileen's generosity.

That night I began thinking about my life and my sons. Stephen had always been a rebel – a heart of gold mixed with a boyish, selfish attitude.

Stephen was, and is, very funny. When he was around fourteen years old, Stephen and a mate of his (who we will call 'Mike Simpson') decided to go with some friends to the home of an older gay guy – who had a reputation for buying booze for young blokes. I guess the guy did this on the off-chance that he might get lucky, but the young lads were well aware of his motives and simply looked on it as an opportunity to score some booze, while carefully avoiding the guy's advances.

So that the guy couldn't contact them again, Mike suggested that they shouldn't use their real names. Everyone agreed. Mike knocked on the door and introduced himself as 'Brian Murray'. Stephen introduced himself as 'Mike Simpson'.

As soon as he could, Mike hissed, 'Why did you use my name?'

Stephen, with a grin, replied, 'You said I shouldn't use my own name!'

When the boys were younger, the three of us did BMX. On one occasion, we had a full-day meet over at Masterton. My parents, who were visiting us, had made us some lovely healthy sandwiches; but when Tony and I returned from our races at lunchtime, the sandwiches were all gone. Stephen had sold them and bought potato chips! That was bad enough, but he'd sold them to some of the kids we'd brought over in our van – so I could just imagine their mothers asking them what they had for lunch, and the kids saying, 'Mr High sold us their sandwiches.'

Another memorable incident happened at the same track, when Tony was around ten years old. It was a two-day meet, and the boys and I decided to camp out on the track with other competitors. We had a small two-man pup tent with three of us inside. As it was summer, the hosting BMX club had arranged to use the local rugby clubrooms for evening drinks and food. I was relaxing and talking with other competitors and their families. The boys kept coming up and asking me for money to buy soft drinks. As the night wore on, I ran out of cash. Tony asked if he could have a sip of my beer, as he was still thirsty. This must have happened a number of times because, in the middle of the night, he woke and told me he felt sick. I scrambled to my feet, frantically trying to find the tent zip so he could go outside but, unfortunately, the projectile vomiting started before I could get the flap open. Pretty soon, the inside of the tent, along with our sleeping bags and clothes, was covered in spray!

Up until the boys were in their mid-teens, BMX proved a great way for us to bond as a family because it was a recreation that we could all enjoy. In fact, they grew out of it before I did, but that forced me into retirement. I felt embarrassed going along with my little bike and helmet and pads, with no kids as an excuse.

In those early years, I struggled to settle into a church. I initially attended an Anglican church in Silverstream. The congregation was elderly, and typical of established conventional churches. Even at the time, I found these traditional churches boring, as the vicar seemed to race through the communion service with no feeling of purpose. You would have thought that a young guy with two small children in tow, turning up to Sunday morning services, would have caused someone to make enquiries or take an interest; but the vicar didn't seem to care and, later that year, he announced his retirement. I had never really considered that religious people might retire.

I remember one evening service, we were all kneeling in prayer (when I say 'all', there were only about six people in church) and the vicar, who was obviously experiencing flatulence, thought he would let out a silent fart. Unfortunately, it was anything *but* silent in the acoustics of that old-style church, where even breathing was amplified. The boys giggled and looked at me, and were about to state the obvious, so I had to tell them to shut up and keep their eyes closed!

When the boys were young, I devised a system to encourage them to do their chores. The idea was to spread the chore-load evenly by having one do all duties one week, while the other would have a week off, and then they would swap. This way, there was no argument about who was meant to do what or when.

To teach them to budget, I wrote down their pocket money in two old cheque account books using the deposit section and, when they needed cash, they would have to write me a cheque and keep a tally of the balance.

My boys soon reached the troubled teens and, in the spirit of tough love, I kicked Stephen out of home at the age of sixteen, because he had become too hard to handle. He boarded with a family in Upper Hutt, and I'll always be grateful to Dave and Shirley for the contribution they made to Stephen's life. Dave was a large, daunting Maori bloke, who quickly gained Stephen's respect at a time when he needed someone to look up to.

But, when I transferred from Wellington to Auckland, Stephen felt he would like to come home and try again. I picked him up from the airport and, although he was getting a little old for it, we hung out at the Rainbow's End amusement park, because he hadn't been there before. He walked a couple of metres behind me, head down and acting staunch. He had never been on a roller-coaster before, so he and I climbed aboard. It crawled its way to the top, then off it went. Straight down. I looked at Stephen and there was this usually tough teenager, with his cool attitude, looking back at me with a look of fear on his face, yelling, 'D....Dad!'

Up in Auckland, it didn't take long for Stephen to slip back into his old ways and, on two occasions, I caught him with marijuana in the house. On the second occasion, I told him that the next time he would be gone.

One evening, I was walking the dogs over my land and I happened to spot something unusual down by the stream. On closer inspection, I discovered a marijuana plot. I thought, *Damn, I'm going to have to send Stephen away again.* Then I noticed a spray water bottle beside the crop, so I took it back to the house and filled it with Roundup weed killer, before placing it back where I found it. Nothing was ever said about this, apart from Stephen storming into the house one evening and slamming his bedroom door behind him. He knew what I had done, but couldn't confront me without incriminating himself.

I continued to 'church-hop', trying to find a happy medium between the ones that bored me, and the alternatives, where everyone kept wanting to hug me.

Stephen and I eventually parted company, going our separate ways. I would always keep track of him and I did the same with Tony. When I didn't hear anything from them, I would just go to an ATM machine, access their bank accounts and transfer all their money into mine. It worked every time. They would soon call me, sometimes within hours, from a petrol station or dairy, wanting to know where their money was!

When I was in Wellington, I enjoyed a Christian church in Naenae, led by Pastor Barry Galloway, who contributed greatly to my Christian walk.

As I rode north, I felt the need to be conscious of the time I had spent with JC. It was fast becoming a past miracle and was losing impact because other things were taking up my thoughts. I could relate to the way many of the ancient prophets had responded after God had enabled them to witness and perform incredible miracles. Take Elijah, for example. We read in 1 Kings 18 about how he performed an incredible miracle, but, by the time we get to 1 Kings 19, we discover that he has lost his faith in God's ability and is running for his life.

It was beginning to sink in that faith really is far stronger than fact. Faith doesn't have a lid on it, faith stretches out into infinity. As JC had explained, fact is the end and the best you can do is build on it, but, to do that, you need faith.

The next morning I arose early to ride to The Store at Kekerengu for breakfast. It was a reasonably moderate ride from there to the Picton Ferry, where I boarded and sailed to Wellington.

As I sat on the ferry, my phone rang. It was Baz from Bularangi Harley Tours. He said that Ali had realised I must have been riding – she was in a little panic as she was try-ing to track me down, and could I give her a call? He and I chatted for a little while and realised how close our paths must have crossed; he was on the road as well – delivering a rental bike to Queenstown.

After hanging up, I was about to ring Ali when my

phone rang again. It was Ali. 'Hey Donks, can you do a ride tomorrow at 1 p.m.? I have a fifty-six kilogram female for a two-hour pillion ride. Her sister and niece bought it for her for Christmas. Kerry was meant to do it, but has opted to take a 112 kilogram male on a different ride instead, which is strange. Please can you do it?'

I said, 'Sure Ali, I'll be there.'

Chapter 12

Immature is a word boring people use to
describe fun people having fun.

I arrived in Wellington that afternoon and headed straight up the island. I was reasonably refreshed after the ferry crossing, and thought I would ride as far as I felt like I could, which happened to be another place I'd stayed at before – with my friends Barry and Lynaire, who own Regent Lodge Bed & Breakfast. I knew it was an easy three-hour ride home from there, so I would be in plenty of time for the Harley Tour.

The next morning, I was on the road at 7 a.m. I gassed up at Wairakei and headed north. I took the Whites Road bypass just north of Putaruru, and stopped for breakfast at O-del-emz in Matamata. From there, it was a short trip home to unpack, wash the bike and shower. My phone rang and it was my mate, Duds, asking if I was back yet. He said that a group of them were meeting at the bike shop and riding SH16, if I wasn't too tired to join them. I explained I had a Harley tour, but that I'd try and meet them if I could. At 12:30 p.m., I put an extra leather jacket in my saddlebag and strapped a spare helmet to the rack, arriving at the Mt Eden address where I was supposed to pick up my pillion passenger, at 12:55 p.m. It was a rest home. *This'll be interesting*, I thought.

They must have heard the bike, because an attractive middle-aged blonde appeared and said, 'Hi, I'm the sister – Glenda. She'll be out soon.' A young girl appeared with a camera and was introduced as Katerina. She explained she was a language student from Germany who was boarding in Glenda's private residence. I pretty quickly cottoned on to the fact that Glenda was the owner of the rest home. A cute little dog wandered out of the house as well, and sniffed at my feet. I bent down to pat it, but it wandered away and was content to investigate the smells of the grass verge. Then, another middle-aged, attractive blonde lady appeared. She had the most amazing sparkling blue eyes and a captivating smile. 'Hi, I'm Denzil,' she said.

I'm uncertain exactly what my reaction was, but I know my heart skipped a beat and my eyes seemed to water. I felt I was holding back tears and was dead scared I was going to cry – which would have completely ruined the expected biker image.

Could this be *the* Denzil who JC had told me about? I felt unusually nervous, and toned down the 'crass biker' routine that usually went with these jobs, as I assisted her with the jacket and helmet.

I did suggest, however, that, after climbing on, she should press her breasts hard up against my back. 'Purely for safety reasons, of course!' I said. She laughed and did as instructed.

I mentioned that a group of Harley guys were meeting up for a ride and asked if she would like us to tag along with them. She thought that was a great idea, so we set off for the bike shop. Unfortunately, Duds and the others had already left by the time we arrived, and I wasn't sure which way around the loop they would ride. I made the decision to head for the Puhoi Pub – a good choice, as it's probably the most popular biker pub in New Zealand.

Denzil hung on tight and we were soon heading north. I took the Silverdale exit and we rode through Orewa. We passed the café where I had first met JC. His bike wasn't there, of course, though I had secretly hoped it would be – if only to stop and say, 'Hey, look who I found?' But, somehow I was fairly sure he already knew.

We arrived at Puhoi and pulled in beside the thirty or so bikes already parked outside. As we took off our helmets and placed them on the mirrors, I quickly put on my cap, not wanting to display my thinning helmet hair. We wandered over to a table and I was greeted numerous times with 'Gidday, Donks' and 'Hi, Donkey'. I think she was impressed that everyone seemed to know me.

Denzil had a red wine and I had a ginger beer. We chatted intently, as if we were attempting to catch up on lost time. As we swapped stories, and she told me a little about herself, I had a sense of déjà vu. It was a completely natural exchange of history, as if I was hearing it for the first time, although I already knew a lot of it. It was a strange feeling.

As we finished our drinks, she said to me, 'Are those your own teeth?' I said they were, but, knowing they check the health of horses by the condition of their teeth, I asked her if she was perhaps taking the 'donkey' thing a little far. She laughed and said that I must look after them. 'Don't worry,' I replied, 'I floss twice a day.' She laughed again and we wandered back to the bike, then set out towards Warkworth.

We turned into Woodcocks Road and, after about five kilometres, I recognised the headlights of eight familiar Harleys heading towards us at speed. My arm went up to acknowledge them and they responded as they passed. In my mirror, I saw Duds' and Blok's brake lights go on as they pulled over. I was told later that they waited on the side of the road for me to turn around, and thought it was strange when I didn't.

Instead, Denzil and I carried on, riding SH16 and down the Northwestern Motorway. As it was late afternoon, I asked Denzil if she had plans for the evening. She said she didn't, so I rode to a place that was, at the time, the Auckland HOG Chapter's favourite hangout – a restaurant called Archies, in Newmarket (great pizzas).

We rode in and I parked on the pathway by the reserve. We took off our helmets and walked over to the restaurant. Archie – the man himself – greeted me with his usual, 'Good evening, Capitán Señor Donkey.' Again, Denzil seemed suitably impressed, and even more so when the cute little European and South American waitresses brought us our menus, saying, in broken English, 'Hello, Mr Donkey.'

Denzil and I chatted eagerly and I was impressed with her directness and no-holds-barred honesty about her life and thoughts. I love people who don't regret the decisions they've made in their lives. Obviously, Denzil had made some great choices in her life, and some – from what I could determine – were very suspect. But, as she said, they were her choices and, at the time, she was fully aware and happy to make them. I asked if she would make some of them again, knowing the outcomes.

She said she doesn't suffer regrets, knowing only too well that you can't turn back the clock; so she just gets on with life and never looks back. I admire that in a person. Too many people rely on past events as an excuse for non-performance and don't attempt to move on.

The rest of the story about Denzil's life, and about Denzil and me, will have to be told in the next book. Perhaps I'll call it something like, *The Continued Adventures of Donkey – Saving Denzil.*

But I will tell you that I explained to Denzil that I couldn't do life without God in it, and noticed that she didn't seem put off by that statement. I told her that I had recently met Pastor Peter Mortlock at the Auckland Harley-Davidson dealership. He and his wife, Bev, were both Harley riders. I told Denzil that Peter was starting up another City Impact Church in Mt Wellington, and that I was planning to go along. I asked if she like to attend with me. She said she would.

During the service, Peter made mention of a couple from Christchurch called Peter and Anne Morrow, who just happened to be the pastors that married Denzil and her late husband, forty years ago. This seeming coincidence blew

Denzil away, and she knew God was speaking to her. I have never heard Peter mention the Morrows in a service, before or since, and Denzil believes it was especially for her.

To cut a long story short, Denzil and I were married in the City Impact Church on the 31st of March, 2012. I sent an open invitation by email to friends and family. Sixty-four Harley-Davidsons escorted us into the church building and 221 people attended – all on the strength of that one email. People even flew in from all over New Zealand and Australia.

Denzil and I knew that we had been truly blessed, and that feeling continues to this day.

Live to learn for the rest of your life
and learn to live for the rest of your life.

epilogue

I didn't see JC face to face all that often after that – some-times I'd think I'd caught a fleeting glimpse of him as he rode by – I'd turn my head or check my mirrors and he'd be gone. But I knew deep down, in some way, he was always with me. The Holy Spirit kept reminding me of the things JC had said, and of the types of things he would say in all kinds of situations.

I'll always treasure those days riding with him around New Zealand and all the things he taught me.

This character they call 'Donkey' has been a bit of a rogue at times. The nickname given to me by my HOG mates gave me a kind of alter ego, and it still does. It allows me to step outside myself and act as Donkey would – gives me a break from being Mrs High's little boy, Peter. If I screw up (which happens often), I often blame it on Donkey. If I say a joke that goes down like a lead balloon, it was Donkey who said it.

JC brought about a new level of work-in-progress maturity and wisdom in me without changing who I am. Everyday I continue to enjoy the new me as my business and friend-base matures and grows along with me, and my relationship with JC continues and extends daily to new levels. God saved Peter High, but he also saved Donkey.

www.ingramcontent.com/pod-product-compliance
Lightning Source LLC
Chambersburg PA
CBHW050007070726
47592CB00018B/1080